CHANGE YOUR HABITS, CHANGE YOUR LIFE

D1470448

CHANGE YOUR HABITS, CHANGE YOUR LIFE

*Strategies that Transformed 177 Average People
into Self-Made Millionaires*

NORTHLOOP
BOOKS

TOM CORLEY

North Loop Books
322 First Avenue N, 5th floor
Minneapolis, MN 55401
612.455.2294
www.NorthLoopBooks.com

NORTHLOOP
BOOKS

ISBN-13: 978-1-63505-004-2
LCCN: 2016900244

Distributed by Itasca Books

Cover Design by Mary Ross
Typeset by Jaad ~ Book Design

Printed in the United States of America

"Tom has taken it upon himself to help society understand the difference between living a rich and poor life. Having studied high and low net-worth individuals for more than a decade, Tom has blessed us with a book that helps us clarify habit formations, the mental functions driving our daily routines, the importance of consistency and how we can turn poor habits into Rich habits whilst coming out on top every single time."

—Jacques van Heerden, founder of the An1ken Group

"Since my discovery of Tom Corley's Rich Habits, I have become aware of the poor habits that keep me from achieving success. Paying attention to the weak areas of my life is the key to making long-lasting, positive changes for myself, my family and my community. It's not easy, and it certainly isn't quick, but making incremental improvements over time has helped me become a better person."

—Steve Stewart, financial wellness coach

"I've always been a huge proponent of habit change. Tom's methods will help you create a drastic change that lasts, instead of falling into the cyclical trap of temporary inspiration and defeat."

—Jordan Harbinger, host of *The Art of Charm* podcast

CONTENTS

ACKNOWLEDGMENTS

NOTHING worthwhile ever gets accomplished without a team of people behind you. This entire Rich Habits journey I've been on these past eleven years has brought me close to some amazing people who I like to think are part of my team. These amazing individuals have helped shine a light on my Rich Habits research. They literally pulled me out of a cave and gave me a microphone.

Darren Hardy, publisher of *SUCCESS Magazine*, was kind enough to interview me for the November 2014 edition, and now nearly 300,000 individuals know who I am and what my Rich Habits are all about. Thank you so much, Darren.

Libby Kane of Business Insider has become one of my favorite cheerleaders. Libby has given me the opportunity to share my Rich Habits research with millions of Business Insider readers. I very much appreciate Libby for opening the door and inviting me in to Business Insider as a contributor. Thank you, Libby, for your incredible support.

Hillcrest Media, my publisher, does such an amazing job editing and producing my books, and they've done it again with this latest book. I appreciate each and every one of the dedicated staff at Hillcrest whose passion for what they do has transformed my books into both bestsellers and award-winning books. Thank you, Hillcrest, for all you do.

I'd also like to thank Paula Andrea, whose feedback helped me refine and improve my book. Paula devoted an enormous amount of time in identifying many ways to improve my book, in particular the discussion on financial success. Thank you, Paula.

INTRODUCTION

I SPENT five years researching the daily habits of 233 wealthy individuals and 128 poor individuals. This research became the basis for my bestselling book, *Rich Habits*, and my award-winning book, *Rich Kids*. This book, *Change Your Habits, Change Your Life,* expands on that research, highlights the most powerful habits that create success, and also includes the latest breakthroughs in the science of habit change. For the first time, this book reveals some of the shortcuts to habit change I uncovered through my research.

No matter what you may believe, you have the ability to change the circumstances of your life. You can go from average to success, mediocrity to wealth. You are not defined by your past or current circumstances. Circumstances can be changed. But in order to change your circumstances you need three things:

1. Daily growth (in skills and knowledge)
2. Focus
3. Persistence

By using the habit-change strategies in this book, you will automatically acquire these three characteristics of success. Habits, by their very definition, are persistent routines. When you adopt good habits, they help you grow your skills and knowledge. Good daily habits enable you to focus every day on pursuing success. They put success on autopilot. Each good habit you add to your life has a cumulative effect. They are like an investment in your individual success. The key is to get your personal Habit Seesaw tipping in the right direction, with your Rich Habits outweighing your Poor Habits. Getting control of your habits is empowering. It gives you a sense of control over your life. According to the latest research on happiness, having a feeling of control over your life is one of the most significant drivers in creating happiness ("General Social Survey", University of Chicago, 2014.) Your new habits will not only put you on the path to success, they will also put you on the path to happiness. Your life will never be the same. Everything is about to change for the better.

UNDERSTANDING HABITS

.

The Purpose of Habits

Habits have a purpose. They save the brain from work and help conserve brain fuel. Habits allow each of us to perform tasks without thinking. Habits are really three things: they are unconscious behaviors, unconscious thinking, and unconscious decisions we make. A golfball-sized area of the brain called the "basal ganglia" governs habits. The basal ganglia resides deep within the brain, in an area known as the limbic system. It is the unconscious command and control center for habits. When the basal ganglia decides that a habit needs to go to work, it instructs the brain to fire up specific brain cells, and once fired, we find ourselves unconsciously engaging in some behavior, thinking, or decision-making. I'll get into this in more detail in the pages that follow.

Unless we force ourselves to become aware of our habits, we will never be able to change our habitual actions, habitual thinking, or habitual behavior. Habits slip right below the radar of our consciousness. Habits are, quite simply, an amazing invention.

Studies show that many of our habits come from our parents, our first important role models. According to these studies, parents have the most influence over the habits we develop in our childhood, and most of these habits we carry with us into our adult years. Parents infect kids with their habits. Some of this parental habit mimicking is neurological. Our brains have something called mirror neurons. The purpose of mirror neurons is to enable babies and children to mimic the behaviors and emotions of their parents. These neurons are ancient relics of prehistoric human evolution, with a primary purpose to aid in survival. Some of this parental mimicking is also environmental. Kids are always tuned in, watching the behaviors of their parents. And lastly, some habits are forced upon kids; for example, when parents mandate and encourage certain behaviors. A study of 50,000 American families, conducted by Dr. Pressman, director of research for the New England Center for Pediatric Psychology out of Brown University (as published in *The American Journal of Family Therapy*, 2014) found that habits in children are unlikely to vary much after the age of nine.

Only when kids become adults are they able to break free from the habits forged during their early lives. Their new habits develop from new environments, career mentors, lifelong self-education, or from the school of hard knocks.

In another study on habits it was determined that an average of 40 percent of all daily human activities are habits ("A New Look at Habits", Wood and Neal, Duke University, 2006). Habits include both physical and mental behavior. These daily habits unconsciously control our lives. Our daily habits, as boring as they may be, are the secret to success, failure, or mediocrity. Our habitual behaviors, both physical and mental, and the choices we make, are the cause of wealth and poverty. Those who learn good daily habits from their parents, a mentor, or through the school of hard knocks, excel in life. Their lives are outstanding. They rule the world.

They command respect, make most of the money in this world, and control the lives of millions who do not have good daily habits. Our daily habits are the reason we live in a beach house or a slum. They are the reason we make millions of dollars a year or eke out a living, forced to live paycheck to paycheck. Our daily habits are the reason we are happy or unhappy. Our daily habits are the reason our children go to the best colleges or struggle to graduate from high school. The blueprint of our life and the lives of our children are determined by daily habits. That's how important habits are. If you want to change your life you must change your daily habits.

Habits and Your Brain

Habits are nothing more than specific brain cells that talk to one another frequently. Frequency is the key. When the brain notices certain brain cells constantly chatting with one another, the brain puts a "habit" label on them. These "habit" brain cells are like little computers that are all linked to another group of brain cells deep inside the brain called the basal ganglia. Imagine how computers are linked in a computer network. The basal ganglia is that golfball-sized mass of brain cells I mentioned a few pages ago. It has many purposes, one of which is controlling habits. Think of the basal ganglia as the central computer for habits. One of its jobs is to oversee habits. When it sees an opportunity, the basal ganglia does one of two things:

1. Labels certain brain cells as "habits"
2. Instructs those brain cells when to begin a habit

When the basal ganglia sees an opportunity to start a habit, it sends a signal to the front part of our brain. It says,

"Engage habit!" The moment the front part of the brain receives this signal, it sends a command and those "habit" brain cells then tell us to engage is some habitual behavior.

Why does the brain do this? Why are habits so important to the brain? Habits save the brain from work, which means the brain uses less energy, less fuel. When the brain engages in a habit, it requires almost no work. It's an unconscious act. This is important because thinking and other conscious acts consume a great deal of glucose and oxygen. Glucose is the fuel supply to every cell in the human body, including the brain. All the food we consume is eventually converted into glucose, or stored for later use in our fat or muscles. Glucose passes through each cell, and once inside the cell it is violently ripped apart and converted to use as fuel. Converting glucose to cell fuel requires oxygen. Each day our little three and a half-pound brains consume 20 percent of the entire body's supply of glucose and oxygen. Unlike the rest of the body, which can store glucose in fat and muscle, the brain can't store glucose. The brain has no readily available supply of fuel to use when it's needed. For this reason, glucose is considered a precious commodity to the brain. Habits reduce the brain's need for this precious brain fuel.

With respect to the brain, habits are an investment. In the beginning of the formation of any habit, the brain invests precious brain fuel in the creation of a habit. This habit creation process is like building a house. A lot of work goes into constructing the house, but once the house is built the construction work ends. Thereafter, it's a matter of maintenance. It's the same thing with habits. Once the habit is formed, the hard work is done and it's thereafter a matter of maintaining the habit. It's very efficient. And the brain likes efficiency. For these two reasons, efficiency and fuel conservation, the brain naturally likes habits, encourages habits, and fights us when we abandon or try to change an existing habit. That is why habit change is so hard—our own brain goes to war with us each time we try to change a habit.

According to a famous study by University College of London, performed on ninety-six people, the habit formation process took anywhere from eighteen to two hundred and fifty-four days, with the average habit taking sixty-six days to form. The study also found more complex behaviors, such as swinging a golf club, required more time for a habit to form. Less complex habits, such as teaching children to brush their teeth every day, could be formed in a matter of days. This study made clear that habits come in many shapes, sizes, and shades, each with a unique level of complexity and influence over our daily lives. The adoption of some habits affects our lives more than others. One powerful habit, in other words, can offset three or more less powerful habits, in terms of the consequences they have on our lives. Smoking cigarettes, for instance, is a bad habit that can negatively offset the benefits of daily exercise and good nutrition.

But who wants to wait as long as two hundred and fifty-four days for a new habit to stick? I don't. You're looking at two hundred and fifty-four days of hell, quite frankly. This is why New Year's resolutions only last a few weeks. The brain eventually forces you back into your old habits. There's a much easier way to change your habits. There are ways we can fool the brain into enthusiastically embracing habit change. But unless you know how to fool the brain into adding or removing a habit, you're going to lose the war, and habit change will be impossible.

In this book I will share with you the unique strategies I uncovered in my research that will allow you to fool the brain into changing your habits. Instead of fighting you on habit change, these strategies will actually seduce the brain into wanting to change a habit. When your brain becomes a partner with you in changing your habits, habit change occurs immediately, which means your life begins to change immediately. Money problems, relationship struggles, work issues, poor health, and many other parts of your life that are just not going well will immediately begin to change for the better once you change your habits.

Habits Can Change Your DNA

Did you know that your daily habits can turn genes on or off? It's known as gene expression, or "epigenetics." Gene expression is a process in which certain genes are turned on or off during one's lifetime. The human body contains approximately 100 trillion cells. Within each cell is the nucleus. Inside every nucleus of every cell are genes. Experts estimate the average human has over twenty thousand genes. Some of these genes are from your mother and some from your father.

Believe it or not, your daily habits can turn genes on or off (Howard, *The Owner's Manual for the Brain*, 2014). Bad habits can turn off good genes and turn on bad genes. This could mean opening the door to cancer, diabetes, various addictions, brain damage, heart disease, etc. Bad habits can create long-term stress in the form of financial problems, job loss, health issues, etc. Long-term stress increases the production of cortisol, a stress hormone. Like a domino effect, cortisol switches on a series of bad genes that can lead to heart disease, cancer, and immunological disorders.

Some of the bad habits that turn on bad genes include:

- Excessive alcohol consumption
- Drug use
- Eating too much junk food (not eating healthy)
- Lack of daily aerobic exercise
- Consuming too much sugar
- Not exercising our brains (for example, by reading or learning new skills)
- Negative emotions and negative thinking

Conversely, good habits can turn bad genes off and turn good genes on. The byproduct of good habits is reduced stress resulting from financial independence, happiness, good health, etc. Some of these good habits include:

- Daily reading or learning new skills, which can turn on genes that increase your IQ
- Daily aerobic exercise, which can turn on genes that prevent heart disease, asthma, and other immuno-logical disorders
- Meditation, which can turn off bad genes that con-tribute to the onset of various types of diseases and turn on good genes that prevent such diseases
- Positive thinking and positive emotions, which alter the brain's chemistry and increase or decrease gene expression

Habits can alter your DNA by changing your genome. This is important not just for you. When you change your DNA you can pass along this altered DNA to your children, for better or for worse.

Habit Formation

Thanks to the amazing research of Charles Duhigg, author of *The Power of Habit*, we have a much better understanding of the process that drives habits, particularly: the cue, the routine, and the reward. The cue represents a familiar environmental point of reference that sends a message to the basal ganglia that it is time to engage in a habit. This is one of the reasons environmental changes can disrupt habits, which we'll get into a little later. Once we are exposed to an environmental trigger, the basal ganglia takes over and directs us to engage in the routine. At the end of the routine is a reward waiting for us. For example: You're driving in the car with your kids and one of them screams out, "McDonald's. I want to go to McDonald's." Your child just noticed the golden arches and immediately began thinking about the delicious chicken McNuggets inside the building behind the golden arches. So you turn right at the golden arches (the cue), pull into McDonald's (the routine), and your kids gorge themselves with McNuggets (the reward).

This process repeats itself with every habit. Instead of golden arches, it might be a pot of coffee (time for the coffee habit) or your Friday routine after work (time for the beer or wine habit) or turning on your computer (time for the check email habit). Every habit has a cue, a routine, and a reward.

Habits are formed over many years of repetitive behavior and thinking. Habits are the byproduct of common brain cells repeatedly talking with one another. Brain experts call this brain cell chatter a "synapse." The more frequent the brain cells talk with one another the stronger the synapse becomes. Brain cells that talk to each other, in a sense, marry one another. They are often stuck with each other for life. Sometimes, when certain brain cells talk to each other enough, the basal ganglia, the command and control center for habits in the brain, will label them as habits. It does this in order to save the brain from work, which also saves the brain from using fuel. Once the basal ganglia labels brain cells as habits, those brain cells remain habits forever. They never get unlabeled. This means you will be stuck with your habits forever—unless you know the secrets to habit change. There are unique strategies that we'll cover in this book that will help you fool the brain into getting rid of habits that are holding you back in life and adding habits that will launch you into another dimension—into the top 5 percent of those high achievers who are wealthy, happy, and successful in life.

Where Do Your Habits Come From?

Where did you pick up most of your habits in life? I'll bet you never gave it much thought. Your habits did not just manifest out of thin air. They came from some source. Each source, good or bad, inspired you to adopt certain habits. The habits we adopt in life primarily come through associations we make in life, our education, our experiences, and our environment. Below is a list of the sources of our habits in their order of influence:

- Parents
- Mentors
- Informal education (e.g., reading books)
- The school of hard knocks (e.g., learning from mistakes and failures)
- Formal education
- Your culture

- Your environment
- Siblings
- Spouse or significant other
- Friends
- Schoolmates
- Fellow workers
- Grandparents
- In-laws (spouse or significant other's family)
- Teammates
- Public figures (celebrities, professional athletes, and famous people)

I'd like to drill a little deeper into the most influential sources of the habits we pick up in life.

Parents

By far the fountain of most good or bad habits we pick up in life is our parents. Many adult habits are forged in childhood. Kids watch what their parents do and then emulate them, good or bad. The self-made millionaires and poor people in my study picked up specific good or bad habits from their parents that unknowingly set them on the path to wealth or poverty in their adult lives. According to my data, 75 percent of the self-made millionaires in my Rich Habits Study learned good success habits from their parents. A recent study by Brown University, in which nearly 50,000 families were surveyed, concluded that habits in children are unlikely to vary after age nine (Rebecca Jackson, "Study Finds Habits in Children Take Root by Age 9," *Psychology Today*, Feb. 26, 2015). Since kids are going to pick up most of their adult habits from their parents, parents can become success mentors to their kids, teaching them good habits that will help them succeed in life. In my study, self-made millionaires had at least one parent who taught them success habits. Let's take a look at a few:

- Warren Buffet: Warren's father was a stockbroker. It's no accident that Buffet became the world's best-known value investor. He was mentored by his dad.
- The Kennedy's: Joseph Kennedy was a very successful politician who mentored sons JFK, Bobby Kennedy, and Teddy Kennedy.
- Ken Griffey, Jr.: Ken, arguably the most talented baseball player ever, was mentored by his professional-baseball-player dad, Ken Griffey (NY Yankees).
- Bill Belichick: Bill's father was a football coach at Navy for thirty-three years. At age three Bill could be found on the knee of his father watching film of Navy football players.

Parents who raise successful millionaire children all have one thing in common: good habits. It's not an accident that their children excel in life. One or more parents taught those kids certain success habits that elevated them above the competition as adults. Parents are often the only shot most have at a mentor in life, which is the next source of habits we will discuss.

Mentors

The second greatest source of your habits comes from mentors. According to my data, 24 percent of the self-made millionaires in my study adopted habits taught to them by career mentors. Of these 24 percent, a whopping 93 percent said that the habits they learned from their career mentors were responsible for almost all of the wealth they accumulated in life. The average wealth of each of the millionaires in my study was $4.3 million. Finding a career mentor, therefore, is like someone depositing millions of dollars into your bank account.

Below is a list of some famously successful people who attributed much of their success in life to specific mentors:

- Oprah Winfrey: mentored by Mrs. Duncan (fourth-grade teacher).
- General Colin Powell: mentored by his father, Luther Powell.
- Dr. Martin Luther King: mentored by Dr. Benjamin E. Mays.
- Henry David Thoreau: mentored by Ralph Waldo Emerson.
- Senator John McCain: mentored by William Ravenel (high school teacher/coach).
- Walter Cronkite: mentored by Fred Birney (high school journalism teacher).
- Gloria Estefan: mentored by her grandmother, Consuelo Garcia.
- Helen Keller: mentored by Anne Sullivan.
- Bob Dylan: mentored by Woody Guthrie.
- Quincy Jones: mentored by Ray Charles.
- Martin Sheen: mentored by Rev. Alfred Drapp.
- Denzel Washington: mentored by Sidney Poitier.
- Rosa Parks: mentored by Alice L. White (headmistress).
- Tom Brokaw: mentored by Frances Morrow (elementary school teacher).
- Mitch Albom: mentored by Morrie Schwartz (Albom is the bestselling author of *Tuesdays with Morrie*).

- Larry King: mentored by Edward Bennett Williams.
- Tim Russert: mentored by Sister Mary Lucille.
- Jack Canfield: mentored by C. Clement Stone, Mark Victor Hansen, Janet Switzer, John Gray, Bob Proctor, Jim Rohn, and John Maxwell.

CASE STUDY ON MENTORING: JAMIE DIMON

Jamie Dimon is one of the most successful, respected bankers in the world. Dimon was mentored by the legendary broker/banker Sandy Weill. The Weill-Dimon team was legendary for how intensely they worked together and how many mega-deals they collaborated on. It was a far cry from the typical employer/employee pairing. In 1983, Weill, then at American Express, hired a young, eager Dimon (whose stockbroker father had worked for Weill) when he was just twenty-six and fresh out of Harvard Business School. Weill left American Express two years later, and Dimon followed his mentor. The two of them worked side by side for many months, studying potential opportunities. Eventually, they found one they liked called Commercial Credit, a struggling lender in Baltimore. The duo took Commercial Credit public, using it as a base with which to build their empire. What followed was a string of mergers culminating in the 1998 merger of Weill and Dimon's companies with financial powerhouse Citicorp which gave birth to the financial powerhouse now known as Citigroup. Dimon benefited enormously from his much older and very wise mentor. Dimon went on to become the CEO of JP Morgan, one of the most powerful financial institutions in the world. When you find a career mentor in life, it puts you on the fast track of success.

Informal Education: Reading Books

Many successful people attribute their success in life to self-help success authors such as Dale Carnegie, Earl Nightingale, Og Mandino, or Jack Canfield. Co-founder of Microsoft and tech icon Bill Gates has made no secret of his passion for books. Gates loves to read, and loves to share what he's reading with others through the Gates Notes blog, full of book reviews, books he's read, and books he wants to share with the world. Beyond recommendations, the Bill & Melinda Gates Foundation has made it a mission to bring more useful technology to U.S. libraries and libraries around the world. On a more personal level, the Gates home stands as a testament to his love of reading, with a 2,100 square foot private library, complete with a domed reading room and a Leonardo da Vinci notebook valued at nearly $31 million.

The School of Hard Knocks

Fifty-one percent of the self-made millionaires in my Rich Habits Study are business owners. Twenty-seven percent of these millionaires failed at least once in business. But like a phoenix rising from the ashes of their failures and mistakes, each rose wiser and wealthier. The school of hard knocks is perhaps the hardest way to pick up good habits. When you run or start a business you will make many mistakes. When you make a mistake in business, it costs you time and money. Because it costs you time and money, the lessons stick. You either figure out what to do and what not to do, or you go under. You become your own mentor through the school of hard knocks. The most successful businesses in the world are built on top of a mountain of mistakes. The more successful you are as a business owner, very likely, the more mistakes you made along the way.

What Triggers a Habit?

Every habit begins with a trigger. Triggers set in motion every habit you have. That basal ganglia we talked about earlier is the command and control center for habits. It is always hunting for triggers in our environment in order to set a habit in motion. As mentioned previously, habits enable the brain to work less. Less work translates into less fuel usage. The basal ganglia, in a sense, is also the brain's fuel efficiency manager, using habits as its main energy-savings device. Once a habit is triggered, you unconsciously engage in the habit. There are six primary habit triggers that set most habits in motion:

1. Visual Triggers

Visual triggers are like external neon-colored billboards that scream at you to engage in a habit. The McDonald's arches are an example of a powerful visual trigger. Beer commercials are another example. Attractive women eating Doritos is yet another.

2. Auditory Triggers

Hearing something can set in motion a habit. When the alarm clock goes off, that's a trigger to wake up and start the day. When we hear an email alert, that's a trigger to check our email. When we hear our baby crying, we know it's time for a diaper change or feeding.

3. Time Triggers

We all have habits that we engage in during the morning, afternoon, and evening. Waking up in the morning is a trigger that sets in motion all sorts of habits: drinking coffee, exercising, brushing teeth, showering, reading, meditating, going to the bathroom, etc. Afternoon triggers set off your afternoon habits: eating lunch, gossiping, reading, surfing the Internet, making personal phone calls, networking, meetings, etc. Nighttime prompts you to engage in nighttime habits: eating dinner, drinking a glass of wine, watching TV, reading, making personal phone calls, exercising, engaging in a hobby or extracurricular activity, gardening, going to a bar, etc.

4. Stress Triggers

Stress can force you to engage in a habit. Stress overwhelms the brain, consuming far too much fuel. To compensate, the basal ganglia is put to work, prodding you to find a habit in order to conserve brain fuel.

5. Association Triggers

People who you associate with are habit triggers. One friend can be a trigger for hitting the bars, another for exercising, another for gambling, yet another for golfing, fishing, tennis, etc. Who you associate with become habit triggers. This is why you should avoid individuals with bad habits. They drag you down by triggering bad habits.

6. Beliefs and Emotions

Our beliefs and emotions trigger habits. Negative beliefs and emotions trigger bad habits and positive beliefs and emotions trigger good habits. If you want to eliminate a bad habit, you need to eliminate the negative belief. In order to do this you must become aware of the negative emotions that trigger negative beliefs while they are occurring; then you must reprogram your belief system from negative to positive. This stops the ensuing bad habit in its tracks.

One of the keys to breaking bad habits is awareness of the triggers that set them off. Identifying the external triggers that set a habit in motion will empower you to break bad habits.

Some examples:

BAD HABIT	TRIGGERS
Eating too much fast food	McDonald's arches, watching TV, snacking habit
Smoking Cigarettes	Access to cigarettes, drinking alcohol, friends, time of day
Gambling	Advertisement, driving by convenience store, having a bookee, friends
Watching too much TV	Time of day

Understanding what triggers your habits requires you become aware of the habits you have as well as the triggers that set those habits in motion. Awareness is the key. Without awareness, habit change is impossible.

How do Beliefs and Emotions Affect Habits?

Beliefs can create wealth or poverty. If you believe you are smart, you are right. If you believe you are dumb, you are right. If you believe life is an oyster, you are right. If you believe life is a struggle, you are right. What we believe determines who we become in life.

The subconscious part of the brain makes up 80 percent of brain processing power. The other 20 percent is the conscious part of the brain. This 80 percent controls the autonomic system, directs behavior, stores habits, and, finally, is where our emotions and beliefs reside.

Our pre-frontal cortex (conscious mind) rarely picks up most of the sensory information we take in every day. Every day we are bombarded with an enormous amount of data taken in by our five senses. The hippocampus and reticular activating system (RAS, part of the subconscious) sees or captures all of this sensory information but intentionally does not share it with the conscious mind. This is so the conscious mind does not get overwhelmed, causing it to go into overload and shut down (meaning sleep). Instead, the subconscious filters what information the conscious mind sees, by way of the reticular activating system. The RAS allows in only certain, specific information. The information allowed into the conscious mind represents three types:

1. Information necessary for survival.
2. Information related to dreams and goals.
3. Information related to our beliefs.

When it comes to survival, the conscious mind picks up a threat through one of its senses and instantaneously relays the potential threat to the hippocampus and amygdalae. If the threat is real, the conscious mind is taken offline during fight or flight and the limbic system and brain stem (part of the subconscious mind) instantly notify the cerebellum (controls motion) to get moving. You see the aftermath of this when victims of some life-threatening accident are said to be in a state of shock because they are unresponsive. What's really happening is their pre-frontal cortex is still in shut-down mode and the subconscious is running things.

When we pursue dreams and goals, the RAS alerts the

conscious mind about certain information it came into contact with, which it perceived as critical in helping us realize those dreams or achieving those goals. When it comes to dreams and goals, the subconscious mind communicates with the conscious mind through intuition and hunches. We call this "the voice inside your head."

With regard to beliefs, the RAS shares information it perceives as consistent with our beliefs. Beliefs represent emotionalized thought programming accepted by the subconscious mind. Each belief represents a mini computer program that came about due to some emotional event. Our beliefs create the lives we live. If we are unhappy with our current financial circumstances, we need to change our beliefs. Our beliefs and our emotions play an important role in habit formation. A belief is formed in two ways:

- Through internal and external programming—self talk (internal) and statements made by others (external) that we have accepted as the truth.
- Through life events anchored in strong emotions.

The people closest to us, our parents, friends, teachers, coaches, etc., are the primary source of many of our beliefs. Some of these beliefs are formed by positive feedback and some are formed by negative feedback. This feedback sticks when it triggers strong positive or negative emotions. If the emotions we experience at the time of the feedback are strong enough, it gives birth to a belief which then alters our behavior: "Tom's a great tennis player." I heard that often and at an early age so it infused me with enormous emotion. As a result I practiced seven to eight hours every day during the summer and hit balls against my basement wall during the winter.

Beliefs can also alter your behavior negatively. "You're

an idiot. If your head wasn't attached to your neck you'd forget it somewhere." My dad said this to me, out of anger, when I was just nine years old. I remember where it was said, when it was said, and how it made me feel—stupid. It became a belief because of the powerful negative emotion I felt at the time it was said. Once I accepted that belief, it triggered all sorts of bad behavior that eventually became bad habits. I stopped doing homework, stopped paying attention in school, and stopped participating in class. Why do homework, pay attention, or participate in school? I'm too stupid to get an A. My new limiting belief eventually caused me to hate school. School only reminded me of my belief—that I was stupid. As a result of accepting this new limiting belief, I adopted habits that caused me to struggle academically for many years.

The amazing thing about beliefs is that no matter how ingrained they are they can be changed. You don't have to be stuck with them forever, as I discovered in the eighth grade. This was when I met Ms. Summers. Ms. Summers was my eighth-grade science teacher. She was so pretty and so nice. All the boys in class had a crush on her, including myself. Early into the eighth grade, I was, surprise, surprise, failing science. After failing yet another test, Ms. Summers asked me to stay after class. She wanted to speak to me. Unfortunately, staying after class had become, for me, a regular occurrence. I just assumed I was going to get another lecture about not working hard, being an underachiever, etc. Instead, Ms. Summers told me that she believed I was very smart and that my problem was that I didn't believe in myself. She did, she said. She believed I could get the highest grade on the next test, if I wanted to. In fact, Ms. Summers went one step further. She told me she believed I was going to get the best grade on the next test.

I remember going home on the bus that day and all I was thinking about was studying for my science test, which was three days away. I studied every night for three days for that damn test. I never studied so hard. I still remember those three days like it was yesterday because of what happened next. When Ms. Summers handed me my test results, in big black numbers was "99." I had received the second highest grade in the class. I couldn't remember getting a 99 on a test, ever. Ms. Summers then called me to the front of the class and spent, what seemed like an hour, telling everybody in my class how smart I was. The emotion, the elation that I felt in not only getting the second highest score but in how Ms. Summers made me feel, is still with me to this day. I felt smart. Ms. Summers was able to shatter my limiting belief because of the strong emotions I felt after doing so well on the test. Ms. Summers caused that emotion by making such a fuss with me in front of the entire class. One person's words changed my life forever because it created new emotional thought programming, also known as a belief. And it all happened in the course of just three days.

I went on to become a solid B+ student the rest of my eighth grade and into high school and college. I was even able to pass the CPA exam, get a master's degree in taxation, and passed the Certified Financial Planning Test, a ten-hour exam, on the first try. The new belief, that I was smart, changed my study habits for the rest of my life.

Your daily habits are determined by your beliefs. If you believe you are smart, you will form good study habits and listening habits. If you believe you are stupid, you will form bad study habits and poor listening habits. Once a belief is accepted, the brain creates habits around that belief in order to streamline activities and behaviors. If you have bad daily habits, the cause is your negative, limiting beliefs. If you have good daily habits it is because you have strong positive beliefs driving those good habits.

Parents, teachers, company managers, and anyone in the position of authority has the capacity to eliminate the negative, limiting beliefs and bad habits of their children, students, and employees. We all need to positively inspire everyone we are in a position to influence. One person can change the entire life of another person by simply altering their beliefs, which will, in turn, rid them of their bad daily habits forever.

Below is a list of some limiting beliefs that are creating bad habits and holding you back in life:

- Poor people can't become rich.
- I'll always have just enough to get by.
- Rich people have good luck and poor people have bad luck.
- I am not smart.
- I am ugly.
- I never have enough money.
- I can't do anything right. Everything I try, I fail at.
- People don't like me.
- I'm disorganized and have no discipline.
- I'm not good at [fill in the blank] (school, work, cooking, reading, relationships, math, science, remembering things, etc.).
- I'm fat because I can't lose weight.

Each one of these limiting beliefs is an individual mini computer program altering your behavior in a negative way. These limiting beliefs are responsible for the life you have. If you are unhappy and want to change your circumstances in life you need to replace these limiting beliefs with positive, uplifting beliefs. It can be done. Here are some powerful strategies that will reprogram your subconscious and completely transform your life. If you follow these strategies for thirty days, the reprogramming will stick and you will shift your mindset from negative to positive.

EXERCISE: WRITE YOUR FUTURE LETTER

Writing the future letter is a lot of fun. It will really get your imagination going. When you're done, you will immediately feel better about yourself. Kids particularly enjoy this activity because it requires the use of imagination. Here's how it works:

Go into the future five, ten, or twenty years. Let's use five years for purposes of this example. Imagine it is five years from now and you are writing a letter to yourself explaining what your life is like. In a perfect world, what would you like your life to look like five years from now? You want to paint a picture of your life, five years from now, that is the perfect, ideal life. It is the life you would want to have if you could snap your fingers today. Describe in your letter where you live, what kind of house you live in, what car you drive, what you do for a living, how much money you make, etc. Describe what you've done the past five years, particularly the goals you've accomplished and the dreams that have come true. This future letter will become the blueprint for your future "perfect" (as self-defined) life.

EXERCISE: WRITE YOUR OBITUARY

This exercise forces you to evaluate your current life and gives you an opportunity to re-write your script for the future. What would you like your perfect obituary to say? How would you like the world to remember you? Include all of the things you would like to accomplish in your life. Don't skimp. List all of the big dreams you realized in your life. Your obituary should make you feel in awe of your life. Really lay it on. Pour out your greatness. Paint a picture of the amazing person you were in life. Like the future letter, let this obituary become the blueprint for your new, amazing life.

EXERCISE: LIST YOUR DREAMS AND WISHES

List every wish or dream that you find in your future letter and obituary. Then reduce it to the top five wishes or dreams you would like to come true over the next five years. I'll cover this in more detail later.

EXERCISE: CREATE GOALS

Goals turn dreams into reality. Only after you've defined your dreams or wishes does the goal-setting process begin. Fifty-five percent of the millionaires in my study set goals around their dreams and wishes. I'll cover this, too, in more detail later.

TYPES OF HABITS

Keystone Habits vs. Ordinary Habits

There are two types of habits:

1. Ordinary habits
2. Keystone habits

Ordinary habits are simple, basic, standalone habits: the time you wake up in the morning, the route you take to work, how you hold a fork, etc. Keystone habits are more unique habits. They are unique because they affect other ordinary habits. Keystone habits act like packmen; they move around searching for and overpowering other ordinary habits. Adopting keystone habits is the key to massive habit change. Let me give you an example:

It's New Year's Day and one of your resolutions is to lose weight. You're about fifty pounds overweight. A close friend, who is a runner, says the fastest way to lose weight is to run. So you decide to start running (keystone habit). You hate running, but after doing it for a while you're down fifteen pounds. One night you attend a social event and someone you know compliments you on your weight loss and tells you how amazing your look. You go home that night feeling happy, like you're floating on air. That compliment triggered an emotion inside of you and really got you pumped up. The next morning you decide to cut back on junk food (ordinary habit) and stop overeating (ordinary habit). You decide to run more in order to lose more weight, so you cut back on smoking (ordinary habit). Adopting just one keystone habit, running, had a domino effect, causing the elimination of three ordinary habits: eating junk food, overeating, and smoking cigarettes. That's why keystone habits are unique and so powerful.

The Many Shades of Habits

Every habit results in an outcome. Some habits cause happiness, sadness, financial success, poverty, good health, bad health, short or long lifespans, etc. There are also habits that alter our IQs, and which affect: relationships, job performance, motor skills, emotions, or our overall circumstances in life. In this chapter we'll tackle some of the major habit categories.

Happiness Habits

You know happiness when you feel it. By definition, happiness is the sustained absence of negative emotions and an ongoing presence of positive emotions. Neurotransmitters are chemicals released when one or more neurons (brain cells) communicates with other neurons. Dopamine is the neurotransmitter for happiness. It is one of sixty neurotransmitters produced by the brain. When neurons release dopamine, it creates a sensation that we call happiness. When our dopamine levels drop below a certain baseline, it creates a sensation we call sadness. If dopamine levels stay below that baseline for more than a few days, we call that depression. Depression is devastating to your health and causes a reduction in energy, which impairs productivity and creativity. When we are depressed, many negative behaviors may set in, such as: we might pull back or retreat from life, we might set down a path of fight or flight (resulting in poor decision-making), we might have increased anxiety, we might become listless, and even get to the point where we lose all interest in life. At this moment almost all activities cease. We isolate ourselves from others. Did you know that depression affects between seven to nine percent of the population (Center for Disease Control and World Health Organization)? It's true. Depression is a widespread, common affliction that affects hundreds of millions of people each year. It's critical, therefore, to engage in habitual activities, both physical and mindful, to maintain or elevate our dopamine baseline in order to prevent sadness and depression from wreaking havoc with our lives.

What activities increase our dopamine levels and vanquish sadness and depression? Let's take a look.

Daily exercise: Humans are genetically hardwired for motion. Exercise sets in motion a domino effect of chemical reactions within the body. We'll get into the importance of exercise in more detail shortly.

Daily learning: We are genetically hardwired to learn. The brain likes novelty. Our inborn natural curiosity is why we are explorers and inventors. Our brain likes it when it's put to use learning new things. When we learn something new, our brains release the neurotransmitters dopamine and serotonin as well as brain-derived neurotrophic factors (BDNFs), a protein and nerve growth factor that is like Miracle-Gro for brain cells. These happiness chemicals are the brain's reward to us for helping it grow brain cells. Reading every day to learn is one of the most powerful happiness activities we can engage in.

Growing constructive relationships: Human interaction is critical to happiness. More importantly, being in good company, surrounding ourselves with other upbeat, optimistic people, elevates our dopamine and oxytocin (another powerful happiness neurotransmitter) levels. Being alone or associating with negative types of people reduces the production of dopamine and oxytocin. Worse, these relationships create stress, which depresses the immune system. A depressed immune system reduces our resistance to colds and infections, causes plaque to build up in our arteries (which leads to heart disease), and turns on various genes that can lead to cancer. Making a habit out of associating with other happy people makes us happy and healthy.

Practiced positivity: Many studies have shown that making a habit of being upbeat, positive, and optimistic makes people happier and more successful in school, sports, and careers. How do you make a habit of positivity? Start your day off with five minutes of meditation. Meditation reduces stress and repairs the physiological damage caused by stress. When we meditate, our brains release healthy neuro-chemicals such as serotonin, dopamine, and endorphins. Starting to sound familiar? These chemicals trigger positive emotions and produce feelings of euphoria and happiness. Blood pressure drops during meditation and reboots the parasympathetic nervous system, which gets digestion back on track. Five to twenty minutes of meditation a day will do the trick. So how do you go about meditating? There are many variations, but keeping it simple is always best.

EXERCISE: PRACTICED POSITIVITY

Close your eyes and count to one hundred. See each number. Let all thoughts pass by like railroad cars along a track.

After you finish your count, visualize your ideal, perfect life. See yourself living this perfect life, with your perfect family, perfect friends, perfect job, and perfect house. See all of your financial worries disappear. See all of your goals and dreams being realized. If you can do this twice a day, once upon waking and once prior to sleep, that is best. All the negative physiological effects of stress will be offset by meditating. You will be better able to think and cope with your day-to-day responsibilities.

Other positivity habits include: inspirational reading, positive affirmations, and meditations (including review of your "dream wish list" and "ideal, perfect future life" narrative). These daily activities prep your mind for positivity and lift your dopamine levels immediately.

Financial Success Habits

It takes time to become a self-made millionaire. Eighty percent of the self-made millionaires in my study became wealthy after age fifty. Somewhere along the line these self-made millionaires learned the secrets to saving and spending. In most cases they stumbled upon some mentor or read some book or watched some TV program or listened to some radio program that gave them the secret habits on saving and spending. The vast majority of people never learn about these habits and spend their retirement years in abject poverty. But that's not you—because you decided to invest your time and money in this book. And I intend on giving you your money's worth. In fact, if you learn nothing from this book but what follows, you will be in possession of knowledge that less than one 1 percent of the population has. This 1 percent is made up of individuals, according to the latest IRS data, who make in excess of $430,000 a year. So let's dive in. What are some of the financial savings and spending habits we should be aware of?

The Bucket System savings strategy: Self-made millionaires make a habit of saving. The more you are able to save at an early age, the more wealth you'll accumulate. The self-made millionaires in my study all set the goal of saving 10 to 20 percent of their income during their pre-millionaire years. I uncovered a very unique savings habit strategy during my research that helped transform one hundred and seventy-five ordinary individuals into self-made millionaires. I call it the Bucket System savings strategy. There are three steps to the Bucket System:

STEP #1. ALLOCATE SAVINGS BY CATEGORY INTO FOUR BUCKETS:

- Bucket #1: Retirement Savings Bucket. This includes 401(k) plans, IRAs, and other retirement plans or retirement-specific products (i.e., annuities).
- Bucket #2: Specific Expense Bucket. This includes a separate checking account, savings account, money market account, or education savings account (i.e., 529 Plan) for major future expenses such as education costs for you or a child, wedding costs, costs associated with the birth of a child, home down payment, etc.
- Bucket #3: Unexpected Expense Bucket. This includes a separate checking account, savings account, or money market account for expenses such as wedding gifts, medical costs, sudden loss of income (unemployment, medical issues, or birth of a child), etc.
- Bucket #4: Cyclical Expense Bucket. This includes a separate checking account, savings account or money

market account for birthday gifts, holiday expenses, vacation costs, back-to-school costs, etc.

You'll need to set up at least one retirement account and three different bank accounts (one for Buckets 2, 3, and 4) in addition to your primary account. If you're saving for education costs for you or your child, you may want to set up a 529 Plan.

STEP #2. ESTABLISH SAVINGS GOALS

In order to make the Bucket System work, you need to establish the overall amount of savings you are able to set aside each pay period. For example, 10 percent of your net paycheck. Then you need to allocate this 10 percent into each bucket as follows:

- 5% (50% of overall savings) into Bucket #1 (retirement).
- 2% (20% of overall savings) into Bucket #2 (specific expense).
- 1.5% (15% of overall savings) into Bucket #3 (unexpected expense).
- 1.5% (15% of overall savings) into Bucket #4 (cyclical expense).

STEP #3. AUTOMATE THE SAVINGS PROCESS

This is where the rubber meets the road: implementation. Automatically direct each of the above savings amounts into each bucket's separate account via automatic withdrawal from your net pay. You will need to instruct your payroll company to set up the automatic funding for each of the four "buckets" (accounts). The payroll company will then automatically send each specific savings bucket amount to the custodial account or bank account that will be accumulating these amounts for you.

That's it. Pretty simple, right? "But I don't make enough to save," you say. Well, I'm here to help. I'll now show you how to cut your spending in order to be able to find the money you'll need to save.

You'll never get rich if you spend more than you make. Here's a list of ten strategies that will help you manage your spending and increase your savings:

1. Track spending: I like to call this "spending awareness." Knowing where your money is going gives you control over your finances. You may find you are paying for things you are not using, such as club memberships or subscriptions.

2. Periodically audit expenses: Many expenses can change over time. Insurance costs often change. They can go up or down over time. Make sure you are paying the lowest insurance rates for homeowners, auto, and life insurance. Cable and Internet costs can increase without you being aware of it. Calling your cable or Internet provider to secure the lowest fees available should be an annual process. Periodically shop cell phone plans. Increased competition in the cell phone industry is driving down monthly rates. Make sure you are not paying more than you have to.

3. Purchase good-quality used cars: New cars lose value as soon as they come off the lot. Buying good quality used cars allows you to take advantage of this loss in value anomaly prevalent in the auto industry. Forty-four percent of the rich in my study

purchased good-quality used cars. Typically these are cars coming off a lease. They may be two or three years old. At 125,000 miles most cars will require some annual repairs. Expect to incur about $1,500 a year in repair costs when you hold on to cars beyond this 125,000 mileage mark. That is still significantly less than you would spend on a loan or lease for a new car.

4. Refinance your mortgage and home equity loans: Are you paying the lowest rate possible on your mortgage? Do you have a home equity loan with a high rate of interest that you can roll into your new mortgage? Can you roll your student loans into your new mortgage?

5. Use coupons: Even the wealthy in my study engaged in this money-savings habit. Thirty-three percent of the rich used coupons to buy food. Why pay more than you have to on groceries or other expenses?

6. Shop at second-hand stores: Many second-hand stores carry high-quality clothing. You may have to spend a few extra bucks on tailoring, but it is well worth the additional cost. Don't let your ego get in the way. Thirty percent of the rich people in my study purchased their clothing from these stores. They didn't let their egos get in the way of spending their money wisely.

7. Downsize your home or apartment: For most, a home or apartment is the most expensive part of the spending budget. Downsizing into a less expensive home or apartment will save you thousands of dollars in interest, taxes, and repairs every year. Keeping your

housing costs to below 30 percent of your monthly net pay should be the goal.

8. Bargain shop: Far too many make spontaneous purchases, paying much more than they otherwise would. That's a Poverty Habit. Shopping for bargains and taking advantage of sales events for planned purchases (needed items) is a smart money habit.

9. Stick to BYOBs: Depending on where you live, there are many restaurants that do not sell alcohol, beer, or wine and allow you to bring your own spirit of choice into their restaurant. Restaurants mark up liquor sales by as much as 100 percent. If your location doesn't allow this, consider having a drink in the comfort of your home before or after the restaurant.

10. Vacation at timeshares: Here's the deal, those who sell timeshares significantly discount the cost of a three- to five-day vacation in order to get you into their timeshare. Your only obligation is to sit through a two- to three-hour sales pitch. Sure, it's a nuisance but it can cut your vacation costs down by 50 percent or more. Is two to three hours of suffering through a sales pitch worth a thousand dollars?

Below are some specific guidelines on how much to spend on ordinary living expenses:

- Pay yourself first: Save 10–20 percent of your net income before you pay anyone else.

- Never charge ordinary living expenses on a credit card: If you can't meet your ordinary living expenses and must resort to the use of a credit card, you are by definition, living beyond your means. Accumulating credit card debt is the third leading cause of bankruptcy, behind a job loss and medical costs.

- Spend less than 30 percent of your net income on housing costs. Housing costs include rent, mortgage, real estate taxes, utilities, insurance, repairs, and maintenance.

- Spend less than 15 percent of your net income on food. This includes groceries and does not include prepared food. Prepared food is part of your entertainment budget.

- Spend less than 10 percent of your net income on entertainment/gifts. This category includes bars, restaurants, movies, music, books, gifts, etc. Eating out and any prepared food you purchase is part of your entertainment budget.

- Spend less than 5 percent of your net income on car expenses. Car expenses include a lease, loan, insurance, gas, tolls, registration fees, repairs, and maintenance.

- Spend less than 5 percent of your net pay on vacations.

- Avoid gambling. If you're going to gamble it should come out of your entertainment budget.

- Don't go over the top on gift giving. Gifts are part of your entertainment/gift budget. Sticking to your 10 percent entertainment budget will prevent you from going overboard on gifts.

- Spend less than 5 percent on clothing. More than a few of the wealthy in my study had the Rich Habit of buying the bulk of their clothes at second-hand or consignment stores. Many of these stores sell high-quality clothing at a deep discount. It may require spending a few more dollars on a tailor, but it's well worth the additional cost.

• Do not spend spontaneously—it is never a good idea. You need to take the emotion out of your spending habits. There is always time to plan and shop before you spend your hard-earned money.

Maintain a spending budget for all of the above spending categories and get into the habit of writing down everything you spend for thirty days. This will open your eyes to how much you actually spend. Real spending is always a very different dollar amount than imagined spending. You will be shocked to find out how much you spend on certain budget categories. And that's a good thing. Getting control of your spending is not an easy task. Once it becomes a daily habit, however, it gets much easier. You will fall into a pattern and a routine that will keep you out of the poor house, enable you to save, and put you on the path to financial independence down the road.

Pretty amazing stuff, isn't it? When you have knowledge, it empowers you and enables you to change your life. But I'm only warming up. There's a lot more I'm going to share with you that will rock your world and set you on the path to success and happiness.

Health Habits

Maintaining your health is critical to living a long, healthy, positive, and energetic life. Here's a list of the healthy habits that will get you there:

Daily exercise: Exercise triggers the release of hormones known as endorphins and also the release of dopamine and serotonin, two powerful neurotransmitters. These chemicals all work in tandem in changing our mood and emotions from negative to positive. If we exercise daily, it is virtually impossible for depression to take root. Daily exercise also reduces stress. Running, jogging, walking, biking, lifting weights, etc., keep us healthy, happy, and energetic. When we feel stress, there is a domino effect of physiology that takes place inside our bodies. When we feel stress, the hypothalamus increases the release of epinephrine and norepinephrine. These hormones make the heart beat faster and prepare the body for fight or flight. If the stress lingers, a gene on chromosome 10, called CYP17, is activated. This gene goes to work to convert cholesterol to cortisol. One of cortisol's side effects, unfortunately, is that it depresses the immune system by reducing the production of lymphocytes (white blood cells). The gene CYP17 also turns on another gene called TCF, which suppresses the creation of a protein called interleukin 2. Interleukin 2's purpose is to put white blood cells on high alert. White blood cells are our main defense against viruses, diseases, germs, and any parasites that infect the body. Long-term stress, therefore, makes us more susceptible to disease. Daily exercise stops the cortisol conversion process in its tracks, thus reducing stress.

Healthy eating: Making a daily habit of eating more nutritious food and consuming less junk food and alcohol improves our well-being, provides adequate protein to the body, keeps our good and bad cholesterol in balance, reduces our blood-sugar levels, and prevents obesity. Certain supplements such as Vitamin D3 improve our immune system. Turmeric has been shown in various studies to thwart cancer. Vitamins E and C are free-radical sponges. They help rid cells of toxic free radicals. Free radicals, if left unchecked, can damage cell walls and create genetic mutations when they collide with the DNA that resides inside the nucleus of every cell in the body. Genetic mutations can lead to cancer. Eating right and reducing the number of calories we consume to less than 2,000 calories a day, helps maintain our health by reducing the accumulation of fat. Fat stores toxins in our bodies. Less fat means less toxins. If you are unsure if you are eating too much, one way to find out is to track what you eat each day for thirty days. Thirty days of tracking the type of food and the number of calories you consume will open your eyes. How much you think you're eating will differ greatly from what you're actually eating. See the appendix for a copy of the Rich Habits Tracking Schedule. Tracking will help you understand how much junk food you are consuming each day. Ideally, you want to keep your junk food intake to less than 300 calories per day. You want to make a habit of eating more fish, more vegetables, more salads, and healthy meats, such as chicken and turkey. Avoid unhealthy meats such as beef, ham, bacon, hot dogs, and sausage. Unhealthy meats impair our cardiovascular system, elevate bad cholesterol, increase accumulation of fat, and are high in calories. Also, while at times more expensive, organic food is free of pesticides and is not genetically engineered. Pesticides are carcinogens (cancer-causing chemicals).

Habits That Grow Your Brain and IQ

Over the past ten years, neuroscience (the study of the brain) has completely changed our understanding of how the brain works. We now know that the brain changes every day. We can rewire our brains (called neuroplasticity) throughout our entire lives, well into our eighties. We also now know that the hippocampus gives birth to thousands of new neurons every day (called neurogenesis). Thanks to the study and mapping of the genome, we've discovered that turning on certain genes can help increase our IQs during our lifetime. We know that IQ can change over time. IQs are not fixed. Just because you were a "C" student at age seventeen with an IQ of 100 doesn't necessarily mean you will stay that way. You can increase your IQ all throughout your life.

Self-made millionaires do certain things every day that continuously improve their brains and increase their intelligence during their lifetimes. These activities increase brain mass by increasing and strengthening existing neural connections and by creating entirely new neural connections. Let's touch on some of the brain-building activities of self-made millionaires.

Daily learning: Every time you learn something new, you re-wire your brain. New neurons are recruited and begin firing with one another (known as synapses). As new neural pathways are created by learning, your brain actually increases in size; your intelligence grows. Eighty-eight percent of the wealthy in my study, long before they struck it rich, formed the daily habit of engaging in thirty minutes or more of self-education reading. This single, simple daily habit alone helped them to increase their cognitive abilities, which contributed to their success much later in life.

Daily aerobic exercise: Aerobic exercise floods the bloodstream with oxygen. This oxygen eventually makes its way to the brain. Oxygen acts like a sponge inside the brain. It soaks up free radicals (cancer-causing elements) and converts these free radicals to carbon dioxide. The blood carries this carbon dioxide to the lungs, which then removes the carbon dioxide from our bodies by exhaling it into the environment. The more we exercise, the more oxygen we take in and the more free radicals are soaked up by this oxygen sponge process. Aerobic exercise also reduces the incidence of obesity, heart disease, high blood pressure, Type 2 diabetes, stroke, and certain types of cancer. Twenty to thirty minutes of aerobic exercise every day has been proven to stimulate the growth of axons and axon branches on each neuron. Recent neurological studies have found a correlation between the number of axons and axon branches inside your brain and intelligence. More axons and axon branches translates into higher intelligence. Aerobic exercise also increases the release of neurotrophins, or nerve growth factor (NGF). NGF stimulates the growth of neurons, helps maintain a healthy coating around every neuron (called the myelin sheath), and improves synaptic communication between neurons. Increased synaptic communication translates into better memory and faster recall. So, daily aerobic exercise feeds the brain, cleans the brain, and increases your intelligence, each and every time you engage in it. Aerobic exercise also boosts your high-density cholesterol lipoprotein (HDL or "good cholesterol") and lowers your low-density lipoprotein cholesterol (LDL or "bad cholesterol"). The result? Less plaque buildup in your arteries. Studies show that people who participate in regular aerobic exercise live longer than those who don't exercise regularly. Healthier people have fewer sick days, more energy, and this translates into more productivity at work. More productivity makes you more valuable to your organization, customers, or clients, which translates into more money. Long-term stress impairs our immune system's ability to fight off viruses, diseases, germs, and parasites. Because aerobic exercise floods the body with oxygen, this increased oxygen reduces the effects of stress on the body. Aerobic exercise is like a double in baseball; it reduces the effects of stress while at the same time reducing stress itself.

Drink alcohol in moderation: Our livers are able to process about two ounces of alcohol an hour (about two twelve-ounce glasses of beer an hour). Anything in excess of that, allows alcohol to enter your bloodstream, which is then carried to your brain. Once alcohol reaches the brain, it infiltrates the glutamate receptors in your synapses, damaging the neurons' ability to fire off signals. If you regularly drink in excess, you are causing long-term damage to these receptors and this can cause permanent damage to your memory and your motor skills. Is it a coincidence that 84 percent of the wealthy in my study drank less than two ounces of alcohol a day? I don't think so. Their moderation in the consumption of alcohol helped them keep their brains healthy, growing, and improving.

Get a good night's sleep: Eighty-nine percent of the wealthy in my study slept an average of seven hours or more each night. Why is sleep so important to brain function? Everyone who sleeps goes through four to six sleep cycles a night. Each cycle lasts about ninety minutes. Each of these sleep cycles is composed of five separate levels of sleep: alpha, theta, delta, rapid eye movement (REM), and then back to theta. For each individual sleep cycle, the first three sleep levels (alpha, theta, and delta) last sixty-five minutes. REM lasts twenty minutes, and the final level of sleep, theta, lasts five minutes. The number of hours you sleep is less important than the number of complete sleep cycles you have each night. Five complete sleep cycles a night is considered optimal. Completing less than four sleep cycles a night, however, negatively affects our health. REM sleep is particularly important, as its primary function appears to be long-term memory storage. During REM sleep, what we've learned the day before is transported to the hippocampus. If we do not complete at least four ninety-minute sleep cycles a night, long-term memory storage becomes impaired. Completing at least four sleep cycles the night after learning new information or a new skill, locks in the new information or new skill. If we get less than four complete ninety-minute sleep cycles the night after learning anything, it's as if the learning never occurred. Sleep helps you remember what you learned during the day.

Make a habit of engaging in new activities: Every time you engage in a new activity and then practice it, you grow your brain. When we regularly repeat new activities, the neurons communicating with each other begin to form a permanent neural pathway, thus growing the size of our brains. It is critical for older people to engage in new activities in order to keep their brains active and prevent brain shrinkage (per the National Institute on Aging), particularly in the frontal cortex. Those who want to "grow" their brains should engage in a new activity and repeat it until it becomes a new skill. This can take anywhere from eighteen days to two hundred and fifty-four days. Each new activity that becomes a skill creates brain mass and keeps our minds active and our brains healthy.

Weight train three or more days a week: Neural stem cells (new brain cells) are born in the hippocampus and either divide into neural cells or glial cells (support cells for neurons). Neural cells are sent from the hippocampus to the dendrite gyrus, which acts like a traffic cop, ordering them to go to specific regions of the brain. Voluntary exercise increases the number of neural stem cells created by the hippocampus. Here's how it works: weight training delivers blood-soaked oxygen to the brain. The more you lift weights, the higher the blood flow. This increased blood flow then feeds the brain with more glucose (brain fuel) and oxygen (which removes free radicals from the brain like a sponge, in effect cleaning the brain). Weight training also increases the production of BDNF (brain-derived neurotrophic factor) inside the hippocampus. BDNF is like MiracleGro for the brain, helping it give birth to more neural cells. BDNF also helps increase the health and size of old neurons. In effect, weight training grows your brain by creating new brain cells and also by maintaining old brain cells. Every brain cell has one axon and multiple dendrites. The axon of each brain cell connects with the dendrites of other brain cells. This is called a "synapse." There is a direct correlation between the number of axons and synapses an individual has and their intelligence. Lifting weights increases the growth of axons, which helps contribute to increased synaptic activity. Anything that increases the number of axons, neurons, and synapses, therefore, increases intelligence (per Paul Manger, professor of health sciences at the University of Witwatersrand, and Seth Grant, neuroscientist at the Wellcome Trust Sanger Institute at Keele University School of Medicine).

Habits that Build Powerful Relationships

Self-made millionaires are very particular about who they associate with. Their goal is to develop relationships with other success-minded individuals. Eighty-six percent of the self-made millionaires in my Rich Habits Study made a habit out of associating with other success-minded people. Some of the individual characteristics self-made millionaires seek include:
- Individuals who are financially successful.
- Individuals with good habits.

- Individuals who are positive, upbeat, and optimistic.
- Individuals who are calm and happy.
- Individuals who are able to get along with others.
- Individuals who do not gossip about others.
- Individuals who inspire and motivate.
- Individuals who are enthusiastic.
- Individuals who take personal responsibility for their lives.

At the same time, self-made millionaires also make an effort to eliminate toxic relationships. Toxic relationships have some of the following individual characteristics:

- Individuals who are always experiencing some type of turmoil.
- Individuals with bad habits.
- Individuals who are negative, perpetually depressed, unhappy, or pessimistic.
- Individuals who are constantly putting out fires.
- Individuals who are perpetually fighting with someone.
- Individuals who gossip.
- Individuals who are dream killers.
- Individuals who lack enthusiasm.
- Individuals with a victim mindset.
- Individuals who blame others for their problems.

Eighty percent of the self-made millionaires in my Rich Habits Study used four relationship-building strategies to grow and strengthen their relationships:

1. Hello call: The hello call is used primarily to gather information on each contact.
2. Happy Birthday call: The happy birthday call keeps your relationships on life support. At least once a

year you are forced to reach out to your contacts to wish them a happy birthday. About 5 to 10 percent of these contacts will reciprocate and call you on your birthday, taking your relationship off life support.

3. Life event call: The life event call is the most powerful strategy because it puts your relationships on steroids. This is a call you make to acknowledge some life event: birth, death, engagement, marriage, health issue, etc. They grow the roots to the relationship tree deeper and faster than any other relationship-building strategy.

4. Networking/volunteering: Networking and volunteering allows you to meet new people and offers the opportunity to showcase your skills in a safe, friendly, and stress-free environment. Developing a networking process is critical to success. When you network the right way, you gain customers, clients, strategic business partners, followers, and networking partners, and this translates into more money. Self-made millionaires are master networkers. Their networking efforts are intended to grow their association with other successful individuals. There are a number of ways these millionaires go about networking:

   - They join networking groups/clubs. BNI International is the most popular, but many self-made millionaires often organized their own unique networking groups.
   - They joined advisory boards of community businesses.
   - They joined local civic groups such as the Lions

Club, Rotary Club, Chambers of Commerce, Knights of Columbus, Optimist Club, or local business groups.

- They did speaking engagements. Speaking engagements are probably the most efficient networking tool available. One speaking engagement can mean thirty or more potential clients/customers or new relationships. Many individuals fear public speaking. One of the common traits among these millionaires is their ability to overcome their fears. Public speaking sets you apart from the masses. It is a competitive advantage.

- They join non-profit groups and eventually get on the board or run one or more committees. Non-profit groups are a very valuable resource for referrals. It allows you an opportunity to showcase your skills and develop long-lasting relationships. Referrals come from every direction—fellow members, vendors, donors, and beneficiaries of the organization. Most board members on non-profits are very successful, wealthy individuals who have strong, powerful relationships. Joining a non-profit grants you access to this treasure trove of valuable relationships of the other volunteers.

When self-made millionaires find someone special, they devote an enormous amount of their time and energy into building a strong relationship with them. Their goal is to grow each new relationship from a sapling into a redwood. They use the Law of Reciprocity to very rapidly turn their new relationships into redwoods. Here's how this law works: each day you dedicate a portion of your day to improving the life of just one of your valued relationships. Spend time each day helping your relationship achieve their goals, improve their careers, or grow their business. Thirty minutes a day is all it takes. Eventually your relationships will become your biggest cheerleaders, best salespeople, and best referral source. This strategy also opens doors to new contacts. Successful people use the Law of Reciprocity every day.

Rich Habits vs. Poor Habits

Forty percent of all our daily actions, thoughts, and choices are habits. Because habits represent unconscious behavior, most of us are unaware that our current life circumstances are the direct result of our habits. Many individuals live paycheck to paycheck, barely getting by. They either scratch their heads, wondering what they're doing wrong, or they play the victim, blaming others for their circumstances in life. The fact is habits are behind all success and all failure. Habits create outcomes. The habits we pick up in life can be either good or bad habits. Good habits automatically put us on a path of success in life. Individuals with good habits do better in school, better at work, make more money, are happier, are healthier, and have a longer lifespan. Conversely, bad habits automatically put us on a path of failure in life. Individuals with bad habits do poorly in school, at work, make less money, are unhappy, unhealthy, and have a shorter lifespan.

Habits represent unconscious behaviors or thinking we engage in regularly. This is a good thing if those habits are good habits. Unconsciously, through our good habits, we are creating a good life: good financial health, good physical health, good mental health, and an overall feeling of happiness. But if we have bad habits, we are creating a life with financial problems, health issues, depression, and unhappiness.

From my research, I discovered that daily habits dictate how successful or unsuccessful you will be in life. By focusing my research on rich people ($160,000 income per year plus $3.2 million or more in net liquid assets) and poor people ($35,000 income or less per year plus less than $5,000 in net liquid assets) I was able to identify common habits possessed by the rich and the poor. This research is important because it gets to the heart of wealth and poverty causation. I learned eight key facts from my study:

1. Daily habits represent 40 percent or more of all our daily activities, our daily thinking, and the daily choices or decisions that we make.

2. Ordinary habits stand on their own and do not affect other habits. They are easier to adopt and easier to change than more complex habits, known as keystone habits.

3. Certain habits are "keystone habits." As I mentioned earlier, keystone habits are unique habits because they affect other ordinary habits. Keystone habits have a domino effect on ordinary habits. They are the most powerful type of habit. They are also harder to adopt and harder to eliminate.

4. There is a cause and effect associated with habits. Habits are the cause of wealth, poverty, happiness, sadness, stress, good relationships, bad relationships, good health, or bad health. Habits impact our lives without our being aware of it.

5. Most of our habits come from our parents. These

habits are "generational," meaning they are passed along from one generation to the next.

6. Rich people have significantly more Rich Habits than they have Poor Habits.

7. Poor people have significantly more Poor Habits than they have Rich Habits.

8. All habits can be changed.

What are some of the Rich Habits and Poor Habits that are creating a good life or a bad life? In my bestselling book, *Rich Habits*, I identify ten keystone habits that separate the rich from the poor. Here are *The Ten Rich Habits*:

1. I will create my own personal daily Rich Habits and follow them each day.

2. I will create goals and form habits around my goals.

3. I will read thirty minutes or more each day for self-education.

4. I will aerobically exercise thirty minutes or more each day.

5. I will devote part of my day strengthening relationships with other success-minded individuals.

6. I will live each day in a state of moderation.

7. I will accomplish 70 percent or more of my daily "to-do" list.

8. I will make an effort each day to be positive, enthusiastic, and optimistic.

9. I will save 10 percent or more of everything I earn.

10. I will control my thoughts and emotions each day.

While these represent the top ten core keystone Rich Habits, in my five-year Rich Habits Study I identified over three hundred behavior habits, thinking habits, and decision-making habits that actually separate self-made millionaires from everybody else. I'd like to share with you some of that data. It will help shine a light on just how important habits are in shaping the life you have today.

So let's get started on a journey. We are going to take a walk in the footsteps of the wealthy. Together, we will peer into the minutia of their daily lives in order to really see and understand the habits that helped transform their lives from ordinary to extraordinary. We will also take a walk in the footsteps of the poor, looking at their habits, because it's equally important to know which habits hold you back in life. You have to see both sides of the coin. I'm going to list each of the Rich Habits and Poor Habits by level of importance in shaping the lives of the rich and poor. Because no one has ever done a study like this, it's going to open up your eyes. Let's pull back the curtain on the habits of rich and poor. Let's be that fly on the wall in their lives. Remember, these habits are listed by the level of impact they have on the lives of the rich and poor.

The Habits of Self-Made Millionaires — Rich Habits

1. Daily self-education reading: Eighty-eight percent of the rich devote thirty minutes or more each day to self-education or self-improvement reading. Also, 63 percent listen to educational audio books or podcasts while commuting back and forth to work. Most did not read for entertainment. In fact, only 11 percent engage in any entertainment reading at all. The rich read to acquire or maintain knowledge. When they read, 58 percent read biographies of other successful people. There are important life lessons to be learned in biographies of people with rags to riches stories. Biographies expose the thinking habits, challenges, and ups and downs of the subjects. Biographies educate. Fifty-five percent also read self-help or personal development books. These books share basic and novel ideas on improving your life in some way. They force you to evaluate what you're doing right and what you're doing wrong. Self-help books provide a sort of best practices for better living. Lastly, 51 percent of the rich read history books. By studying history, we are able to better understand life. History paints a picture of human triumphs and human failings. It's like a compass, pointing us in the right direction, while also showing us the wrong direction.

2. Thirty minutes or more of daily aerobic exercise: Seventy-six percent of the rich aerobically exercise thirty minutes or more every day. Aerobic exercise involves anything that's cardio: running, jogging, walking, or biking. Any exercise that gets the heart rate up to seventy-five to one hundred beats per minute for twenty minutes or more is considered cardio exercise. Cardio not only is good for the body, but it's good for the brain. Cardio improves brain function. It grows the neurons (brain cells) in the brain. It feeds the brain with certain hormones, like brain-derived neurotrophic factor (BDNF). BDNF is like MiracleGro for brain cells. It helps them grow more dendrites and increases the size of axons, two critical components of brain cells. The more dendrites you have and the bigger your axons, the smarter you become. Cardio exercise delivers more oxygen-soaked blood to the brain. Oxygen helps improve the functioning of brain cells. The more oxygen we take in through cardio exercise, the healthier our brains become. Exercise also increases the production of glucose. Glucose is brain fuel. The more fuel you feed your brain, the more it grows and the smarter you

become.

3. Build relationships with other success-minded people: You are only as successful as those you frequently associate with. If you want to be more successful in life you need to surround yourself with other success-minded people. You also need to minimize contact with toxic people. Successful people can open the door of opportunity to you with one phone call, email, or meeting. You can find these success-minded people on boards and committees of nonprofit organizations. This is why so many wealthy people volunteer for charitable organizations, civic groups, or trade groups. It helps them expand their network of other success-minded people. If you are not rich, volunteer. If you are unemployed, volunteer. If you hate your job, volunteer. The new relationships you will create will open the door to unexpected opportunities. Seventy-two percent of the wealthy volunteered five hours or more each month. 86 percent of these self-made millionaires devoted time to building strong, long-term relationships with individuals who had a positive, upbeat mindset. The rich are always on the lookout for individuals who are goal-oriented, optimistic, enthusiastic, and who have an overall positive mental outlook. They also make a point to limit their exposure to toxic, negative people, which we've already touched on. In my research I discovered the rich spend more than one hour a week with their positive relationships and less than an hour a week with their toxic relationships. You want to maximize the time you spend with your success relationships and minimize the time you spend with your toxic relationships. To build these relationships, the rich do six things: #1 they make happy birthday calls, #2 they make hello calls, #3 they make life event calls,

#4 they network, #5 they volunteer, and #6 they participate in formal or informal mastermind groups. Formal mastermind groups include trade groups, business groups, and common interest groups. Informal groups include weekly or monthly meetings or phone calls with a select number of individuals who are all pursuing something in common, whether a similar goal, similar business, or similar activity. The informal mastermind groups typically have no more than five or six participants. A real-life example of this is found in the car industry. Many new-car dealers within the same franchise make a habit of meeting quarterly to compare notes and share best practices.

4. Pursue your own goals: Eighty percent of the wealthy in my study were obsessed with pursuing goals. Fifty-five percent spent a year or more in pursuit of a single goal. Pursuing your own goals is the key. Too many make the mistake of pursuing someone else's goal. Parents, who want the best for us, may push us to become doctors, CPAs, attorneys, or engineers. Many follow their parents' advice only to find out, years later, that they are unhappy and not making the money they thought they would make. I'm here to tell you to avoid putting your ladder on someone else's wall and then spending the best years of your life climbing it. Find your own wall, your own dreams, and your own goals—and pursue them. They need to be yours and not someone else's. Only then will you find your true calling and some meaning in life. When you pursue someone else's dreams or goals you may eventually become unhappy with your chosen profession. Your performance and compensation will reflect it. You will eke out a living, struggling financially. You simply won't have the passion that is necessary for success to happen.

Passion makes work fun. Passion gives you the energy, persistence, and focus needed to overcome failures, mistakes, and rejection. It infuses you with a fanatical tenacity that makes it possible to overcome obstacles and pitfalls that block your path. According to my data, pursuing your own dreams and goals creates the greatest long-term happiness and results in the greatest accumulation of wealth. Those who pursue their own goals or life dreams, love what they do for a living and are the happiest people.

5. Dream-set then goal-set: There's actually a process to realizing your dreams. Unfortunately, many well-meaning personal development experts don't fully understand the process and, as a result, those who embrace their teachings soon find themselves discouraged and disillusioned when they fail to realize their dreams. The confusion is in misinterpreting goal-setting as the process to realizing your dreams. While goal-setting is part of the process, the actual foundation for realizing your dreams begins first with dream-setting. I'll explain this dream-setting/goal-setting process in more detail soon.

6. Avoid time wasters: When most people think of risk, they think of it in terms of some financial investment they make: investing money in a new business, investing in stocks, gambling, playing the lottery, or lending someone money in exchange for some future financial gain. But financial risk is not the greatest risk you take. You can always earn more money. There is another type of risk that we all take that can never be recouped. It's gone forever. And that risk is time. When we invest our time in anything, it's lost forever. It never gets renewed or returned to us. Yet, because we are all given what seems to be an abundance of time, it

has very little value. So we spend an enormous amount of our time engaged in wasteful activities, such as sitting in front of a TV for hours, commenting on Facebook, watching YouTube videos, sitting at a bar, lying in bed, or engaging in some other non-productive activity. When we waste time, it's gone forever. We don't consider how precious time is until we are older and realize our time is running out. Time needs to be invested wisely—pursuing goals, dreams, or some major purpose in life. Any investment of our time should pay dividends down the road in the form of creating happiness: financial security, a legacy, or the improvement of others' lives. When you see time as the greatest risk of all, it will force you to become more aware of exactly how you invest your time. Invest it wisely, because you will never get it back. Sixty-seven percent of the self-made millionaires in my study watched less than one hour of TV each day. Sixty-three percent spent less than one hour a day on the Internet (recreationally). This freed up time for them to pursue their goals, read, learn, exercise, volunteer, and network.

7. Sleep seven to eight hours every twenty-four hours: Eighty-nine percent of the self-made millionaires in my study slept seven hours or more each night. Sleep is critical to success. Neuroscientists have made some incredible breakthroughs in the past ten years. One thing they continue to study is why we need to sleep. What they are discovering is fascinating. Sleep accomplishes so many things behind the scenes. One purpose of sleep is memory formation. During REM sleep, the hippocampus and neocortex send signals back and forth to each other thousands of times. This process creates memories. Another discovery is that sleep enables offline communication between the

conscious mind (aka neocortex), which shuts down during sleep, and the subconscious mind (limbic system and brain stem). This is important because the subconscious mind is regularly taking in sensory data that is invisible to the conscious mind. When we experience intuition, this is actually the subconscious mind communicating something to the conscious mind during sleep. When you wake, the conscious mind, that voice inside your head, talks to you about what it learned from the subconscious mind while you slept. The average adult requires between six to seven and a half hours of sleep each day, in four to five ninety-minute sleep cycles. Four sleep cycles is a minimum, with five being optimal. Each sleep cycle is composed of five levels: alpha, theta, delta, rapid eye movement (REM), and then back to theta. The first three sleep levels last sixty-five minutes. REM lasts twenty minutes, and the final level of sleep lasts five minutes. Four sleep cycles a night gets you six hours of sleep a night and five sleep cycles gets you seven and a half hours of sleep a night. Some individuals are able to function on six hours of sleep each night and others need seven and a half hours of sleep a night. The number of hours you sleep is less important than the number of complete sleep cycles you have when you sleep. Four sleep cycles is the minimum, while five sleep cycles is optimal.

8. Get up early: Forty-four percent, or roughly half of the self-made millionaires in my study, woke at least three hours before their work day actually began. Why is getting up early so important to success? Life has a way of throwing wrenches into our day. How many of us raise our hands in frustration at the end of a work day because the three or four things we wanted to get done were somehow

replaced by unanticipated disruptions. Unanticipated disruptions happen. Sometimes they happen too often. These disruptions have a psychological effect on us. They can drip into our subconscious and eventually form the belief that we have no control over our life. Once formed, this belief puts on its work hat, telling us, subconsciously, that we are not in control of our day. This belief causes us to feel helpless. Feeling helpless is the number one common cause of depression. But there's a solution. There's a way to take back control of your life and kill the roots to that negative belief. It's called the "Five AM Club." Getting up at five in the morning to tackle the top three things you want to accomplish in your day allows you to regain control of your life. It gives you a sense of confidence that you, indeed, direct your life. It gives you a feeling of power over your life. It puts the reigns of "your" life back into "your" hands. Getting up at five is a daily habit. It will take time to form this daily habit. This is one of those Keystone Habits I like to talk about. Keystone Habits are the most powerful type of habits because of the domino effect they have on other habits. One strategy to help you develop this habit is to find someone to join your Five AM Club to hold you accountable. Someone who will be there, waiting and looking for you at five every morning. This will force you to overcome the urge to sleep in. Start your 5 AM Club tomorrow. Find an accountability partner, someone who will join your Five AM Club. You'll regain control of your life and it will make you feel better about yourself. You'll gain confidence that life is within your control and it will end your feeling of helplessness.

9. Develop multiple streams of income: Self-made

millionaires do not rely on one singular source of income. They develop multiple streams. Three seemed to be the magic number in my study. Sixty-five percent had at least three streams of income that they created prior to making their first million dollars. Diversifying sources of income allows you to weather the economic downturns that inevitably occur. These downturns are not as severe when you have multiple streams of income. Most people have "one pole in one pond" and when that single income stream is impacted by an economic downturn, they suffer financially. Conversely, the rich have "several poles in different ponds" and are able to draw income from other sources when one source is temporarily impaired. Some of the additional streams include: real estate rentals, real estate investment trusts (REITs), tenants-in-common real estate investments, triple net leases, stock market investments, annuities, seasonal real estate rentals (beach rentals, ski rentals, lakefront rentals), private equity investments, part ownership in side businesses, financing investments, ancillary product or services and royalties (patents, books, oil, timber), etc.

10. Avoid procrastination: Procrastination is a Poor Habit. It prevents even the most talented individuals from realizing success in life. Most people have this Poor Habit, and it is not an accident that most people financially struggle in life. Success has many moving parts and procrastination is a big moving part. One of the main contributors to procrastination is not being passionate about what you do for a living. That's 87 percent of the working population in the world. According to Gallup, only 13 percent of employees are "engaged" in their jobs, or

emotionally invested in their work and focused on helping improve their organizations. The data, which is based on nationally representative polling samples in 2011 and 2012 from more than one hundred and forty countries, showed that 63 percent are "not engaged"—or simply unmotivated and unlikely to exert extra effort—while the remaining 24 percent are "actively disengaged," or truly unhappy and unproductive. Why? The reason is that we simply like to do the things we like to do and we put off the things we do not like to do. Whether you realize it or not, procrastination is a big reason why you are struggling financially in life. It damages your credibility with employers and fellow colleagues at work. It also affects the quality of your work and this affects the business you or your employer receive from customers, clients, and business relationships. Procrastination brands you as someone who cannot be trusted or whose work product is poor. Worse, procrastination can lead to litigation, which causes stress and financial costs that can run into the thousands of dollars. Believe it or not, the voice of procrastination screams just as loud and clear in the minds of those who excel in life as it does in the minds of those who do not. The difference is how successful people stop that voice of procrastination in its tracks. In my five-year study on the daily habits of the rich and poor, I uncovered five tools that can help anyone silence the voice of procrastination forever.

5 Tools to Silence Procrastination

Tool #1. To-do lists: Successful people rely on "to-do" lists to help them get things done. There are two types of daily to-dos:

- Goal To-Dos: These are daily tasks tied to monthly, yearly, and long-term goals. These are almost always fixed in nature, meaning the same to-dos show up every day on the to-do list. For example: "Make Ten Telemarketing Phone Calls."
- Non-Goal To-Dos: These are to-dos that are unrelated to any goals. They may be administrative tasks (i.e., Respond to Emails), client tasks (i.e., Meet with Client), or daily obligations (i.e., Go to Bank). They may be fixed tasks, daily tasks, or they may vary daily.

Tool #2. The Daily Five: Every day, successful people incorporate into their daily "to-do" list five things to accomplish before the day ends. This is a particularly important tool for that 87 percent who are not passionate about their jobs. The Daily Five can represent five things that are unrelated to your nine-to-five job. They can be five minor things that you do every day that move you forward toward accomplishing some goal or realizing some dream or purpose in life.

Tool #3. Setting and communicating artificial deadlines: When you set deadlines and communicate those deadlines to third parties who are directly affected by your completion of a task, you increase the urgency for completing the task. It elevates it from a mere "to-do" to a personal promise you make to another individual. It puts pressure on you to fulfill your promise and meet the deadline.

5 Tools to Silence Procrastination

Tool #4. Accountability partners: An Accountability Partner is someone you meet with regularly (weekly, for example) who holds your feet to the fire in accomplishing your tasks. This can be one or more individuals. Knowing that there are others who will hold you accountable to perform certain tasks, elevates those tasks from mere "to-dos." We all perform better when we know others are watching.

Tool #5. "Do It Now" affirmations: No one likes to be nagged. Nagging, whether we realize it or not, alters our behavior. We tend to get something done that we don't want to do when we are repeatedly nagged about it. The "Do It Now" affirmation is a self-nagging technique that works. By repeating the words "Do It Now" over and over again, we are effectively nagging ourselves. When I uncovered this tool during my research, I began using it to nag myself into doing things I regularly procrastinated on, like my company's monthly billing. Now all I have to do is think about the affirmation in order for the nagging to alter my behavior and force me to get that task done.

11. Find a success mentor: Ninety-three percent of the self-made millionaires in my study who had a mentor in life attributed their enormous wealth to their mentors. Sixty-eight percent said that the mentoring they received from others was a critical factor in their success. Success mentors do more than simply influence your life in some positive way. They regularly and actively participate in your success by teaching you what to do and what not to do. They share with you valuable life lessons they learned either from their

own mentors or from the school of hard knocks. Finding a mentor puts you on the fast track to wealth accumulation. In my research I discovered five types of success mentors:

PARENTS

Parents are often the only opportunity to have a mentor in life. Parents who are success mentors to their children help distance their kids from the competition. They set their children up for success as adults. This is why parenting is so critical to success in life. Teach your children good daily success habits. Doing so makes it highly unlikely that they will financially struggle in life.

TEACHERS

Good teachers are good mentors. Teachers can reinforce parent mentoring that children receive at home or step in to provide much-needed success mentoring (particularly when absent at home).

CAREER MENTORS

For those not fortunate enough to have had parents or teachers who provided success mentoring, finding someone at work to act as a mentor is the fast track to wealth accumulation. Career mentors help you avoid mistakes and point you in the right direction. Find someone at work you admire, trust, and respect; then ask them to be your mentor. They should be at least two levels above you at work.

BOOK MENTORS

Books can take the place of actual mentors. The best sources for book mentors are biographies of self-made millionaires.

Fifty-eight percent of the self-made millionaires in my study read biographies of other successful people.

SCHOOL OF HARD KNOCKS MENTOR

When you learn good daily success habits through the school of hard knocks you are essentially your own mentor. You teach yourself what works and what does not work. You learn from your mistakes and failures. This is the hard way because those mistakes and failures carry significant costs in both time and money. But this is also the most effective type of mentorship, because the lessons you learn are infused with emotion and never forgotten

The Habits of Self-Made Millionaires continued . . .

12. Maintain a positive mental outlook: Long-term success is only possible when you have a positive mental outlook. In my research, positivity was a hallmark of all the self-made millionaires. Fifty-four percent of the millionaires believed their optimism had been a driving force in their success. Forty-three percent believed they would one day be rich. Seventy-nine percent believed they were the cause of their circumstances in life. Most of us are completely unaware of our thoughts. If you stop to listen to your thoughts, to be aware of them, you'd find most of them are negative. But you only realize you are having these negative thoughts when you force yourself to be aware of them. Awareness is the key. The Buddhist often refer to this as "mindfulness." Physiologically, these voices inside your head emanate from an area of the brain called the amygdala. The amygdala resides in the limbic system. It never stops talking to us. It's there for a purpose. Think of it as a radar system, warning us

of danger. It broadcasts worry, fear, and doubts as a means of protection, to keep us alert and on guard for danger, predators, unsavory people, etc. This voice whispers to us all sorts of things when we embark on some new, unchartered territory or anything that involves risk. The real-life triggers for this voice include setting goals, pursuing a dream, investing your money in a business or a project, pursuing a new job opportunity, going for a possible promotion with challenging responsibilities, getting married, getting divorced, buying a house, selling a house, moving to a new location, having a baby, going to college, taking up a new sport, etc. Sometimes this voice says things to us like:

- You could fail, lose money, get fired, or go bankrupt.
- You could get hurt or injured.
- You'll embarrass yourself.
- It might not work out; it'll end in divorce; it could be a disaster.
- I'm not up to it; it's too much responsibility for me; what if I do a terrible job?

These negative voices are warnings to stop what we are doing and reverse course back to our comfort zone. Most individuals give in to the voices. But I found a few who don't. These courageous individuals ignore the voices to instead pursue goals, dreams, new business opportunities, and new challenges in life. How? How come they don't obey the voices inside their head? What do they do to overcome these voices and persist, while most everyone else stops in their tracks? The self-made millionaires in my study play the What If? game. The What If? game silences negative voices inside your head. The What If? game diffuses negative self-talk. It's like battery acid, melting away doubt, fear, anxiety, and worry. It is used by some of the most successful individuals, businesses, and research organizations in the world. It is essentially a brainstorming game played in an effort to come up with new products, services, and at times revolutionary breakthroughs.

CASE STUDY: THE WHAT IF? GAME

In his book, *Think Like a Champion*, Donald Trump explains how he shuts down his "demon voices" by playing the What If? game. When Trump is considering a new project, as he confessed in his book, those demon voices come charging in like an army. Many of the demon voices come from inside his head, but many of them also come from individuals who work with Trump. According to him, in the early phases of pursuing a new project these voices warn him of all sorts of dangers. For example, when he was in the evaluation phase of what became his award-winning TV show, *The Apprentice*, Trump was confronted with an overwhelming number of demon voices advising him to stop:

- The show might fail. If the show is a flop, it will damage the Trump brand.
- It will distract me from my current business. My core businesses will suffer financially.
- What if the show turns people against me?
- What if I hate doing the show?

But Trump played the What If? game to direct his thoughts:

- What if the show is a success?
- What if the show helps improve my brand?
- What if I love doing the show?
- What if it helps me make more money?

- What if it helps me find apprentices who are out-standing and can add value to my business?
- What if millions of people around the world fall in love with me and my Trump organization?

The What If? game stops negativity in its tracks and replaces it with positivity. It defuses all of the fears, doubts, and uncertainties we face when pursuing something new or worthwhile. It immediately changes the way we think. It gives us courage to move forward. The next time you are faced with a difficult decision, play the What If? game. Don't give in to those demon voices. What if the demon voices are just wrong?

13. Script your life: Self-made millionaires do not stumble into success. They are not passive beneficiaries of some in-credible stroke of good luck. The journey toward success al-ways starts with a vision. A vision of the person you want to be and the life you want to have for yourself and your family. Sixty-one percent of the self-made millionaires in my study engaged in something I call "dream-setting." Dream-setting involves scripting your ideal future life. In this process, you define your future life, the future you, by imagining all of your dreams coming true; then you put it to paper in five hundred to a thousand words. This is the future letter strat-egy we covered previously. The future letter toggles on the reticular activating system (RAS) as well as the hippocam-pus. Once you turn on the RAS and the hippocampus, they go to work, behind the scenes, searching for ways to at-tract what you desire in your new, future life. They are like drones, programmed to find a target. In this case, the target is anything that will help you realize your dream. Your senses are programmed by the RAS to pick up any input from the

outside world that will get you to your final destination. This data is then filtered through the hippocampus, which decides if this information will help you in achieving goals or realizing a dream. In a real sense, when the RAS is turned on, it allows you to see for the first time. Your eyes open up to opportunities that were always there.

14. Pursue your passion: One of the common threads among all of the self-made millionaires in my study was a passion for what they did for a living. They were among the fortunate few who found their calling in life. Every wealthy entrepreneur in my study who realized incredible wealth also had passion. Passion changes your beliefs about yourself. It infuses you with energy, persistence, focus, and patience. Each one of the wealthy entrepreneurs in my study had an intense desire to realize their dreams. They had a never-ending focus on achieving their dream. They did not let obstacles get in their way. They believed in themselves. Their passion made miracles happen. These self-made millionaires all had six common traits: passion, persistence, focus, patience, a hard work ethic, and a desire to learn. What's even more interesting is that, according to these wealthy individuals, they never knew they possessed those traits until they decided to pursue a dream. Pursuing that dream set in motion all of their success traits. Passion has a domino effect on other success traits, bringing them to life. Passion trumps education. Passion trumps intelligence. Passion trumps working capital. Passion trumps skills and years of technical proficiency. Passion trumps any advantage those who lack passion might have in life. Those few who find passion in something, simply blow the doors off those who lack passion. It is not even a competition. Passion occurs when you find your

main purpose in life. Having a main purpose is the key. It is the magic, secret ingredient to success because it makes passion possible. When you find your main purpose in life, you know it. It's not something you ponder. It hits you over the head like a hammer. You never wonder if you've found your main purpose in life. If you have any doubt, rest assured you haven't found your purpose in life. When you are following your main purpose in life you become a slave to it. The passion it creates becomes all consuming. But how do you find your main purpose in life? Believe it or not, finding your main purpose in life is within your control. Here's the process:

- Take out a sheet of paper and draw five columns.
- In the first column, make a list of everything you can ever remember that made you happy in life. Hopefully, this will be a long list.
- Now highlight those items on your list that involve a skill.
- In the second column, assign a job-type designation to each of the highlighted items.
- In the third column, rank each of the highlighted items in terms of happiness, with number one being the greatest happiness and number two the next greatest happiness and so on.
- In the fourth column, rank each of the highlighted items in terms of income potential, with number one being the highest income and number two being the next highest and so on.
- In the fifth column, total columns three and four. The lowest scores represent your main purpose in life. Here is an example:

MAIN PURPOSE

DESCRIPTION	JOB CATEGORIES	HAPPY	$	TOTAL
When I ran the campaign for class president	Politician, Campaign Manager, Professional Speaker	1	3	4
When I organized the ski trip for our high school class	Event Planner	2	2	4
When I coached basketball in college	Basketball Coach	3	4	7
When I worked part-time in college selling cars	New Car Salesman, New Car Dealership Owner	6	1	7
When I wrote for the school newspaper	Journalist, Author	4	5	9
When I was part of ROTC in high school	Military Career	5	6	11

Once you've identified a number of possible activities that could become your main purpose in life, the next step is to engage in one of the activities for six months. If after six months you do not become obsessed with the activity, move on to the next activity. You know you've found your main purpose in life when you have no choice but to engage in the activity every day. You become obsessed. It is all you think about. Your main purpose is something that you just know you will do until the day you die. You will know that you found your main purpose in life when the activity does not feel like work. While engaged in pursuing your main purpose, time flies by. Before you know it, hours have passed. You will know you found your main purpose when you are infused with passion. Passion makes work fun. Passion gives you the energy, persistence, and focus needed to overcome failures, mistakes, and rejection. According to my research data, finding your main purpose in life creates the greatest long-term happiness and also results in the greatest accumulation of wealth. Those who pursue their own purpose in life love what they do for a living and are the happiest people. Making money becomes secondary to the joy you get in performing the activity that is your main purpose. Ironically, you will make more money than you ever imagined because, through repetitive practice, you will become expert in your craft. You will know you've found your main purpose in life when you are happy engaging in the activity and look forward to waking up in the morning to do the work that makes you happy.

15. Persistence: Self-made millionaires are persistent. They never quit on their dream. They would rather go down with the ship than quit. Twenty-seven percent of the self-made millionaires in my study failed at least once in business. And then they picked themselves up and went on to try again. They persisted. Persistence requires doing certain things every day that move you forward in achieving your goals or life dream. Persistence makes you unstoppable. No obstacle, mistake, or momentary failure will stop you from moving forward. You learn to pivot and change course, growing in the process. Persistence allows you to learn what doesn't

work and continuously experiment until you find what does work. Persistence is the single greatest contributor to creating good luck. Those who persist, eventually get lucky. Some unintended consequence emerges. Some unexpected, unanticipated event happens to those who persist. Sometimes, those closest to you will urge you on and encourage you. But more often, those closest to you, those directly impacted by the obstacles, mistakes, and failures that are part of the success journey, will try to stop you from persisting. It takes almost superhuman effort to achieve success when there are so many forces aligned against you. That's what makes successful people so special and so rare. If you want to be successful in life, you must persist in the face of seemingly unending adversity. Successful people are successful because they never ever quit!

16. Don't follow the herd: What do Facebook and Google have in common? The answer is The Herd Doctrine. Humans have a herd mindset that is simply overpowering. It's what drives teens to engage in certain peer-driven behavior. It's also what made Facebook and Google possible. People simply want to blend in; they want to be part of the herd. We are all hardwired that way, genetically. It's a byproduct of the evolution of the human genome. During the early part of our human existence, we quickly discovered that when we were part of a herd, we were safe from predators. The Herd Doctrine ensured the very survival of our species. We so desire to blend in, to acclimate to society, to be a part of the herd, that we will do almost anything to avoid standing out in a crowd. It's not theory. It's science (Estrada, "How Peer Pressure Shapes Consensus, Leadership and Innovations in Social Groups," *Scientific Reports*, 2013, Macmillan

Publishers Limited.). Many years ago, *Candid Camera* decided to test this science in their famous "Elevator Prank" (www.maniacworld.com/peer-pressure-on-the-elevator.html). In this skit, an innocent bystander is followed onto an elevator by a group of *Candid Camera* pranksters. Once the elevator starts moving, the pranksters all turn around, facing the opposite side of the elevator. The innocent bystander is clearly agitated by this. After a few moments the innocent bystander turns in the same direction of the pranksters. The pranksters then turn around once again and the innocent bystander does the same thing. They repeat this prank with many other innocent bystanders, and the result is always the same: the innocent bystander eventually follows the herd. As funny as that *Candid Camera* prank is, it highlights the lengths people will go to be part of the herd. If you are pursuing success, what you're really trying to do is create or grow your own herd and then get other individuals to join your new herd. There are two parts to The Herd Doctrine.

HERD METHODOLOGY: PART ONE

You must separate yourself from the herd. Failure to separate yourself from the herd is why most people never achieve success. The herd stops them in their tracks. The moment anyone in your herd gets wind that you are pursuing some big goal, life dream, or purpose, they pounce on you. You are bombarded with all sorts of negativity.

"What happens if you fail?"

"Maybe it's too risky."

"The odds of success are stacked against you."

"You're not smart enough."

"Where will you get the money?"

It takes super human effort to persist in the face of such criticism. Most don't. They surrender to the herd.

HERD METHODOLOGY: PART TWO

You must create your own herd and get others to join it. Successful people succeed because they are able to create their own new herd and then draw the attention of others, pulling them into their own new herd. Those who are enormously successful are able to get other herds to move to their product or service. When this happens it is as if these new "herd creators" realize overnight successes, even though it likely took them many years for the other herds to join their new herd. When you succeed in getting others to move to your new herd, you win. For example, when the Facebook herd was formed, a small number of individuals began joining the Facebook herd. Soon, word got out and more joined. Eventually millions who felt left out of the herd began quickly jumping on the Facebook herd bandwagon. That herd has now grown to over a billion members. The founders of Google did exactly the same thing. They were able to move millions from other herds such as Yahoo and AOL to their new herd. Millionaires have big herds, deca-millionaires have bigger herds, and billionaires have huge herds. The bigger your herd, the more successful you will be.

Understanding The Herd Doctrine is critical to success in life. You want to separate yourself from the herd, create your own herd, and then get others to join it. In the beginning, it's a lonely journey. It takes time to get others to notice you. But if you have a good product or service and are persistent, your herd will grow and you will reap enormous rewards. Getting others to join their own new herd is what millionaires and billionaires do. Successful people are actually herd creators and herd movers.

17. Good etiquette: You have to know how to act and how to do certain things when you're around people. Self-made millionaires have mastered certain rules of etiquette that help them in social settings. Here are a few of the etiquette principles you have to master if you want to be a success:

THANK YOU CARDS

Saying thank you is a reflection of your character. When someone sends you a gift, send them a thank you card. Don't Facebook them, Tweet them, Instagram them. Send a thank you card. When should you send a thank you card to someone? When someone remembers your birthday. When someone acknowledges an important life event, such as a death in the family, birth, wedding, engagement, etc. When people refer a customer or client to you, send them a thank you card. When people do you or a direct family member a favor, send them a thank you card. After paying a friend or family member back who has lent you money, send a card. When someone acknowledges an accomplishment or achievement, send a card. When someone does anything good for you or a direct family member, they deserve a thank you card. When someone opens the door to an important contact for any reason or promotes anything that is important to you or a direct family member, send them a thank you card.

PROPER COMMUNICATION

Look everyone in the eye for no more than five seconds at a time, then divert your glance for another five seconds. Practice will turn this into a habit. Not every thought that comes into your head should come out of your mouth. Vet your thoughts. Speaking your mind does not mean sharing every thought. Some thoughts are not appropriate and could cause irreparable damage to your relationships. Never criticize, condemn, or complain about anyone to anyone else. It's a giant red flag. People will assume that you are also bad-mouthing them and will avoid you. Never gossip. Most gossip is bad, negative, and damages relationships. Gather as much information about your relationships as you can. At a minimum, gather the following information: birthdays, hobbies, interests, schools attended, childhood home towns, current family background (married? kids?), current place of residence, dreams or goals, etc. The more you know about people you engage with, the more ammunition you'll have in your arsenal to help you in effectively communicating with them. Make hello calls, happy birthday calls, and life event calls.

DINING ETIQUETTE

Believe it or not, most people don't know how to eat. Many grow up eating while they watch TV or sit at a table in a fast food restaurant. In the adult world of the high achievers, you need to know how to eat at social settings. Here's what you need to know: As soon as you sit in your chair, take the napkin off the table and drape it over your lap. Never begin eating until everyone has their meal. Never chew with your mouth open. Never talk while you're chewing food. Never dip any food you're eating into a sauce everyone is using. Don't wolf down your food. Eat at the same pace as everyone else at the table. Never hold a spoon, fork, or knife with a closed fist. Outside fork is for salads, inside fork for the meal. Never make gestures while your utensils are in your hands. Never reach for anything (not even the salt and pepper!); instead, always ask someone to pass things like that. Don't slouch at the table. Sit straight up. After the meal, excuse yourself; then go to the bathroom and make sure you don't have any food in your teeth. Carry a toothpick or something similar in your wallet or purse wherever you go.

APPEARANCE ETIQUETTE

You have to learn how to dress in life. There's a certain way to dress for work and job interviews. You're going to go to all sorts of social events: weddings, formal dinners, informal dinner parties, engagement parties, funerals, birthday parties, picnics, etc. You need to know how to dress. Here's a basic rundown:

- Work and Job Interviews: Some professions have special-purpose clothing, like construction, roadwork, etc. If you work in an office, dress like your boss or your boss's boss. In some offices its business casual. In others it's a suit and tie for men. For woman, its suits, dress slacks, skirts, collar shirts, blazers or dress shirts with blazers/cardigans, and dress shoes.
- Weddings, Wakes, Funerals: In most cases this will be suit and tie for men. For women it's the same as work clothes but many women like to wear more formal gowns or a more stylish cocktail dress, usually worn with dress shoes. Some cultures have special dress codes you need to be aware of.
- Formals: Formals are black tie optional, black tie or white tie for men. "Black tie optional" means a tuxedo or a dark suit, black tie or bow tie, and dark shoes. "Black tie" means black tuxedo, dark shoes. "White tie" means black tailcoat, white wing-collar shirt, white bow tie, black shoes for men. For women, "formal" means a long formal gown, suit,

skirt with blazer or blouse, or short cocktail dress; all usually worn with dress shoes or heels. White tie events are rare.

INTRODUCE YOURSELF PROPERLY

In life you will be forced into situations where you will meet new people. This is an opportunity to develop valuable relationships. Some may be your next employer, future spouse, next best friend, future co-worker, investor, or future business partner. There are a few basic rules in making introductions: Smile. Offer a firm handshake. Make eye contact. In one sentence, explain who you are, why you're there, and who you know at the event. Ask questions about the person you are introducing yourself to.

BASIC MANNERS YOU MUST HAVE

There are some fundamental manners you will need in order to make yourself respectable in front of others: Say please and thank you. Don't interrupt someone while they are talking. Don't roll your eyes when someone says something you disagree with. Don't look away when someone is talking to you. Never check your cell phone when talking to someone. Stay positive and keep criticisms and negative comments to yourself. Compliment, compliment, compliment. Thank those hosting an event, dinner, etc. Never curse or use inappropriate language during social events. Never be rude.

The Habits of Self-Made Millionaires continued . . .

18. Mentor others: We talked about the importance of finding a mentor but I found in my research there is another mentoring Rich Habit that is almost as important, and that

is mentoring others. Mentoring other individuals makes you more expert at what you do because it forces you to teach what you've learned. Teaching is always the best way to learn anything. Mentoring others also pulls those you mentor into your herd and creates a devoted following that will pay dividends for the rest of your life.

19. Seek out cheerleaders and avoid booleaders: Negative, destructive criticism will derail you from pursuing success. As Charles Schwab, former president of Carnegie Steel, said so many years ago: "I have yet to find the man, however exalted his station, who did not do better work and put forth greater effort under a spirit of approval than under a spirit of criticism." Don't get me wrong: criticism is necessary for success. You need feedback from others. But all too often that feedback is mired in negative, destructive criticism that lacks any real specific constructive advice. "The reason you're not selling more is your product is terrible." Or, "You're bossy, arrogant, pompous, or (fill in the blank)." Or even, "You're failing because you're bad at what you do." And sometimes, "You're doing it all wrong. You need to change what you're doing." While most of this may be true, it lacks any constructive, specific feedback. You're wasting your time listening to it. Most criticism you will receive is, unfortunately, going to be this negative, generalized destructive type of criticism and not the positive, specific constructive type you need. These booleaders offer only negative criticism because they, themselves, have little to no idea how to help you. They've never succeeded in doing what you're doing, so their advice must be general and lack any specific, constructive feedback. This type of negative, destructive criticism only brings you down; it deflates you, slowing you down or

stopping you on your path to success. When you are pursuing a dream, big goal, or your purpose in life, you absolutely must seek out only those who offer positive, specific, constructive criticism. You need to seek out cheerleaders and avoid booleaders. Cheerleaders offer constructive feedback that will help you succeed. Their criticism has tremendous value because they know what they are talking about. Their knowledge is valuable because they have a track record of success in doing what you are attempting to do. They may also have a track record of helping others like you succeed. They have gravitas by virtue of their previous success. If you want to succeed in realizing your dream, you must surround yourself with cheerleaders and avoid booleaders.

20. Believe in yourself: Our beliefs can either create wealth or create poverty. If you believe you are smart, you are right. If you believe you are dumb, you are right. If you believe life is an oyster, you are right. If you believe life is a struggle, you are right. What we believe determines who we become in life. Your beliefs are programming you picked up in life. Much of it was created in your youth, influenced by your parents, siblings, and your environment. These programmed beliefs we acquire in childhood, follow us into adulthood. Some beliefs are positive and others negative, limiting beliefs. The positive beliefs enable us to achieve. Limiting beliefs hold us back, preventing us from realizing our full potential. Beliefs are stored in our conscious and subconscious mind. They are scattered about in the limbic system, the cerebral cortex, our prefrontal cortex, and in many of the hundred billion neurons that make up the brain. Beliefs represent mini computer programs, which direct your behavior, choices, and decisions in life. If you want to change your circumstances

in life, you must change your beliefs. You need to adopt positive beliefs and erase negative, limiting beliefs. Here are some strategies to help you do that:

FUTURE LETTER STRATEGY

We already went over this strategy in detail, but just to recap: The future letter strategy asks you to go out into your future and write a letter to yourself about how amazing your life is. You're basically creating a blueprint of your ideal, perfect life. You describe: where you live, what cool stuff you own, vacations you go on, the amazing work you do that you love, etc.

OBITUARY STRATEGY

We went over this one previously but just to remind you, the obituary strategy asks you to write a few words about the amazing life you lived. You include all of your amazing accomplishments and successes. You want to paint a picture with words of a life that leaves you awestruck.

LIST YOUR WISHES AND DREAMS

I'll cover this in much more detail later in the book but let me give you a little preview here. Once you have completed your future letter and obituary, you then list every wish or dream you find in them. Then reduce your list to the top ten wishes and dreams you find. This list will be your springboard for creating goals around those wishes and dreams.

CREATE GOALS AROUND YOUR WISHES AND DREAMS

Once again, I cover this in more detail in the dream-setting and goal-setting discussions later in the book. The fundamental principle here is to build individual goals around each of your wishes and dreams and then tackle each goal, one at a time.

21. Help others succeed: Helping other success-minded people move forward in achieving their goals and dreams, helps you succeed. It's the "birds of a feather flock together" metaphor. The more success-minded people you help in achieving their goals and realizing their dreams, the more devotees you add to your life. No one realizes success without a team of people behind them. Successful people become successful because they are able to create a valuable support team of other success-minded people. The best way to create your team is to offer help to other success-minded people first. But just don't give help to anyone. There's a reason I am using the phrase "success-minded people." You want to focus on helping only those who are pursuing success, are optimistic, goal-oriented, positive, and uplifting. This is an important point because most people are not optimistic, goal-oriented, positive, uplifting people. Only about 30 percent will meet this criteria (Raj Raghunathan, PhD, *Psychology Today*, 2013). So you need to be very selective; take your time selecting those you want to help.

22. Make thinking a daily habit: "Five percent of the people think; ten percent of the people think they think; and the other eighty-five percent would rather die than think." — Thomas Edison

One of the things that stood out from my Rich Habits Study was how important thinking is to self-made millionaires. I tracked ten different types of thinking habits these millionaires engage in frequently, if not daily. From my research, it was so evident that thinking is key to their success, so I decided it needed to become one of the ten keystone rich habits.

When self-millionaires think, they often do so in isolation, closed off from the world. Most engage in their daily thinking habits in the morning, some during their commute in their car, others in the shower, and still others at night. Morning seems to be the most dominant timeframe, however. Typically, immediately upon waking, these self-made millionaires find a quite space and think. How long? In my study it ranged from fifteen minutes to thirty minutes. What did they think about? Well, they thought about a lot of things and when they thought, they thought in a way that most would call "brainstorming." They spent time every day brainstorming with themselves about numerous things. I was able to boil down those brainstorming sessions into ten core rich thinking habit categories. Here they are:

1. CAREERS

Some of the questions they asked themselves included: What can I do to make more money? How can I increase my value to my clients, customers, or my employer? What do I need to do in order to gain more expertise? What additional skills do I need? What things should I be reading more about? Do I like what I do? What do I love to do? Can I make money doing what I love to do? Should I change careers? Should I work more hours? Should I work less hours? Do I work hard enough? Am I lazy? What am I really good at? What am I really bad at? Does my job make me happy?

2. FINANCES

Do I spend too much money? Am I saving enough money? Will I have enough to retire? How much do I need to retire?

Do I have enough set aside for my kids' college? How much do I actually spend each month? Should I create a budget? Should I revise my budget? Am I doing a good job investing money? Is my spouse doing a good job investing money? Am I paying too much in taxes? Do I have enough life insurance? Should I set up a trust for my kids?

3. FAMILY

Do I spend enough time with my family? Can I work less and spend more time with my family? Am I spoiling the kids? Am I too hard on the kids? Can I get away for a vacation this year? Am I doing enough to help the kids succeed? How can I improve my relationships with my spouse and kids?

4. FRIENDS

Do I have enough friends? Do I spend enough time with the friends I have? Why don't I have many friends? How can I make more friends? Is my work interfering too much with my social life? Do I call my friends enough? How often should I stay in touch with my friends? Who haven't I spoken with in a while? Do I have good friends? How can I end my friendship with so and so? Should I help my friends financially?

5. BUSINESS RELATIONSHIPS

What can I do to improve my business relationships? Am I staying in touch enough with my key customers and clients? How can I develop a business relationship with so and so? Which business relationships should I spend more time on and which ones should I pull away from? Do my customers and clients like me? Do they think I do a good job?

6. HEALTH

Am I exercising enough? Should I lose more weight? Do I eat too much? Am I eating healthy? Should I get a physical? Should I take vitamins/supplements? I need to get a colonoscopy. Are my arteries clogged? Do I get enough sleep? Do I drink too much? I have to stop smoking. I have to cut back on junk food. I need to eat more vegetables.

7. DREAM-SETTING AND GOAL-SETTING

In my study, most of the brainstorming involved personal, financial, family, and career dreams and goals: dreams of retiring on a beach, buying a boat, expanding business, buying vacation homes, etc.

8. PROBLEMS

Here the participants in my study brainstormed primarily about finding solutions to those problems that were causing them the most stress at the moment. Most were immediate problems related to their jobs and their family. Some were longer term and related to preempting future potential problems they were anticipating down the road (most often related to their careers).

9. CHARITY

What other charities can I get involved in? Am I doing enough for my church, business group, synagogue, etc.? How can I best help my community? What can I do to help my grammar school, high school, college, etc.? Should I start a scholarship? Should I contribute more money to my school, church, etc.? Who can I help?

10. HAPPINESS

Am I happy? What is causing me to be unhappy? How can I eliminate those things that are making me unhappy? Is my spouse happy? Are my kids happy? Are my employees or staff happy? How can I make myself happier? What is happiness? Will I ever be happy? What's making me so happy?

That's a lot of thinking, I know. There are a lot of days in the year, however, to brainstorm. You just need to make it a daily habit. Eventually, over time, you will come up with solutions to your most pressing problems. You will gain insight into what makes you tick. Daily thinking will help you find some meaning to your life. Making a daily habit of thinking is what self-made millionaires do. It's an important piece of the success puzzle. Understanding why they do it is less important than understanding that they do it. Every day.

The Habits of Self-Made Millionaires continued . . .

23. Ask for what you want: Fear holds most back from asking for something from someone else. Actually two types of fear: fear of being rejected and fear of obligation. Self-made millionaires overcome these fears and make a habit of asking everyone they can for help. A few of the millionaires in my study said they figured out some people really do want to help and that asking for help was a numbers game. Some will say no, but some will say yes and offer to help. I personally struggle with this rich habit. Let me tell you how I overcame these fears recently. *SUCCESS Magazine* was profiling me in their November 2014 edition, and it dawned on me that I might not have enough money to meet the demand for books (I was self-published). It took me three weeks to muster the courage to make my first phone call to a millionaire

to help fund the book sales. For three weeks I dragged my feet. I was consumed with fear and doubts. But I knew from my research that self-made millionaires, despite their fears, ask for help. So I did. Much to my surprise the first millionaire I called was willing to front me $150,000 to meet the demand. It's the fear of rejection and the fear of obligation that prevents us from asking for what we want. You have to get over those fears and keep asking until someone says yes, if you want to be successful in life. As the Bible says, "Ask and you shall receive." There's a lot of wisdom in that saying.

24. Avoid negativity: While we already discussed the need to avoid negative, toxic people, there is a broader need to avoid any and all negative influences. These often come from people but they may also come from the media: TV, Internet sites, newspapers, radio, magazines, books, and podcasts. Don't spend too much time reading, watching, or listening to news. News is constructed to be negative because negativity taps into our natural-born fears. While you need to stay current with events, it is a bad habit to immerse yourself in news. Reading the news will shift your thinking from positive to negative almost immediately. It causes anxiety, stress, sadness, and in some cases depression.

25. Take calculated risks: Self-made millionaires are able to overcome their fear of failure and take calculated risks. These risks are not without cost. During the journey toward wealth accumulation, many lose money. All of the self-made millionaires in my study invested their own money and most took on debt from banks, family, and friends in pursuit of their dreams. Twenty-seven percent actually experienced failure in their ventures and had to start all over. The

important point here is that they did start over. They failed, made mistakes, and used the lessons they learned from these failures and mistakes to help them to ultimately succeed. The pursuit of wealth requires that you take risks. Most don't, and that's why most are not wealthy.

26. Seek feedback: Fear of criticism is the reason we do not seek feedback from others. But feedback is essential to learning what is working and what isn't working. Feedback helps you understand if you are on the right track. Seeking criticism, good or bad, is a crucial element for learning and growth. It also allows you to change course. The most successful self-made millionaires piloted new ventures before they dove in with both feet. Piloting a new initiative, either by engaging in it on a part-time basis or on a limited basis, provides valuable information that you can use when you decide to go for it; in other words, to devote all of your resources and time to the venture. Feedback provides you with the information you will need in order to succeed in any venture.

Habits That Hold You Back From Success — Poor Habits

Poor habits will make you unhappy, unhealthy, and negative. They will cause depression, relationship problems, and financial struggles. All habits cause outcomes and poor habits create negative outcomes in your life. In order to transform your life, you need to adopt good habits and eliminate bad habits. The rich habits are unique good habits because they were constructed to be keystone habits. What makes keystone habits unique is their ability to stop poor habits in their tracks. Adopting one rich habit has the effect of eliminating many poor habits. That's why the rich habits are so powerful. Each one you adopt is like a double or triple in baseball. It moves you toward success much faster. But in order to know which rich habits to adopt, you need to first identify your own individual poor habits. Below is a top ten list of some of the worst poor habits that are dragging you down and creating a life of misery:

1. Gambling: In other words, the pursuit of success without the sweat. There is no such thing as getting rich quick. Financial success takes time, takes initiative, and requires relentless effort. Those who gamble are deluded into thinking there is a shortcut to success. Fifty-two percent of the poor in my study gambled on sports at least once a week and 77 percent played the lottery every week. Self-made millionaires don't gamble. In my study, 84 percent did not bet on sports and 94 percent did not play the lottery. The odds of gambling and winning are infinitesimal. Self-made millionaires don't pursue any get-rich quick schemes. Instead, they make a habit of pursuing their dreams and their goals.

2. Drinking too much alcohol: Fifty-four percent of the poor in my study drank more than two glasses of beer, wine, or alcohol each day. Eighty-four percent of the self-made millionaires in my study drank less than that. Worse, 60 percent of the poor in my study got drunk at least once a month. Drinking clogs neuro-receptors on brain cells, causing them to misfire, or not fire at all. This affects your memory and ability to think clearly. Drinking also adds significant calories to your daily diet and, over time, will cause you to become overweight or obese.

3. Watching too much TV: Seventy-seven percent of the poor in my study watched more than an hour of TV every

day. Sixty-seven percent of the self-made millionaires in my study watched less than an hour of TV every day. Watching TV is a time waster, and the inactivity associated with it is bad for your health. Facebook, Twitter, You Tube, and other newly emerging social media platforms are replacing TV-watching habits, but they are poor habits just the same. Making productive use of time is a hallmark of self-made millionaires. Wasting time is a hallmark of poor people.

4. Negative mindset: Seventy-eight percent of the poor in my study had a negative mindset. Fifty-four percent of the self-made millionaires in my study had a positive mindset. You cannot succeed in life if you have the poor habit of thinking negative thoughts. When you see everything in your life in a negative way, you will attract more negativity into your life. Once again, this is the brain's reticular activating system (RAS) and hippocampus at work, seeking to provide you with a reality that is consistent with your thoughts. Thinking, "I don't make enough money," is a directive to the RAS and hippocampus to go to work behind the scene, diligently nudging you to do things that will make sure you don't have enough money. "I have bad luck," puts them to work seeking bad luck. "Nothing ever goes my way," will put the RAS and hippocampus to work 24/7 making sure everything goes wrong in your life. "People are mean," makes them look for mean people for you to associate with. "I don't trust anyone," is a directive to these two parts of the brain to find untrustworthy people. "Rich people are evil," virtually ensures that you will never become rich. "I'm poor because I was born poor," is a negative limiting belief that programs the RAS and hippocampus to make sure you stay poor.

"I can't afford (fill in the blank)."

"I'm not smart or educated enough."

"It's not my fault I'm poor."

"The rich or the government is causing my poverty."

"Life is a struggle."

I can go on and on. You get the point. When you allow negativity to rule your thoughts, you are programming your brain for failure. You'll have no chance in life at breaking out of your current financial or life circumstances. These negative thoughts will become beliefs that act like computer programs. Worse, if you have children, they will adopt your negative thinking and struggle in life as adults. This is why the saying "the poor get poorer" has so much truth to it.

5. You don't read: Ninety-two percent of the poor in my study did not read to learn. Seventy-nine percent of those who did read, read for entertainment. Success requires growth. That growth comes from reading and educating yourself on a daily basis. If you want to succeed in life you must engage in daily self-improvement reading.

6. You have toxic relationships: Only 4 percent of the poor in my study associated with success-minded individuals. Ninety-six percent associated with negative, toxic individuals. You are only going to succeed in life if you surround yourself with the right type of people.

7. One stream of income: Poor people have one income stream. Their eggs are all in one basket. Typically, that one stream of income is a job. If they lose that job, they lose their only source of income.

8. No life plan: Ninety-five percent of the poor in my study had no life plan. They never took the time to develop a

blueprint for their future life. Success is a process. It starts by developing a script of the life you desire. This script becomes your blueprint for success. It helps you define your long-term goals. Without a blueprint, without long-term goals, we are like leaves on a fall day, floating in the air aimlessly.

9. You spend more than you make: Ninety-five percent of the poor in my study did not save and most accumulated debt to subsidize their standard of living. Consequently, they have no money for retirement, for their kids' college, or for pursuing opportunities that present themselves. Eighty-eight percent owed more than five thousand dollars in credit card debt. Not saving and spending more than you make creates long-term poverty, with no hope of escape.

10. Poor health habits: Seventy-seven percent of the poor in my study did not exercise. Ninety-seven percent ate more than three hundred junk food calories each day. Sixty-nine percent frequented fast food restaurants three or more times a week. Eighty-six percent did not floss daily. Sixty-nine percent ate candy more than twice a week. Fifty-three percent got less than seven hours of sleep each day. Sixty-six percent were thirty pounds or more overweight. Poor health habits create detrimental luck. This is a type of bad luck that is the byproduct of poor habits, poor behavior, and bad decision making. Detrimental luck caused by poor health habits can result in diabetes, heart disease, cancer, high blood pressure, or any number of diseases or disabilities.

Do any of these poor habits sound familiar? Not to worry. I will show you exactly how to eliminate your poor habits and create your own personalized daily rich habits. Each individual has their own specific poor habits that are holding them back. The key to transforming your life is to eliminate old poor habits and replace them with new rich habits. I will show you exactly how to do this.

The Habit Seesaw

Now that we've had a chance to better understand the difference between rich habits and poor habits, it's time to talk about the Habit Seesaw. Visualize a seesaw. Now imagine on one side of your seesaw are all of your rich habits and on the other side are all of your poor habits. If you want to be wealthy, more than 50 percent of all your daily habits must be rich habits. If you are poor, this is because more than 50 percent of all your daily habits are poor habits. If you are stuck in the middle-class, this means that you have a 50/50 split of rich habits and poor habits on your Habit Seesaw.

Getting your seesaw to tip in the right direction, toward wealth accumulation, may be as simple as changing a few daily habits. For example, if you are in the middle-class and you want to become wealthy, you only need to add two or three rich habits, or you only need to eliminate two or three poor habits. If you are poor and you want to become wealthy, you will have to add a few more rich habits and/or eliminate a few more poor habits.

The point I want to make here is that the difference between being rich or poor is not much. It requires only a few minor changes to your daily routine. As mentioned previously, 40 percent of all our daily activities are habits. This means 40 percent of the time we are all on autopilot. Forty percent of the time we don't even think about what we are doing during the day. We are all in zombie mode 40 percent of the time. Now, if you have good daily habits, then this is a good thing. But if you have bad daily habits, then this is a bad thing. Without much thought you are either on the path to creating wealth or poverty. Daily habits are responsible for your wealth, poverty, happiness, and unhappiness. The key is to get that Habit Seesaw tipping in the right direction, and I will show you exactly how to make that happen.

CREATING HABITS AROUND DREAMS AND GOALS

Dream-Setting

Self-made millionaires do not rely on fate, random good luck, God, or the benevolence of others to secure the life they desire. They take action. Successful people shape the course of their own lives. There are a number of strategies they use to create a blueprint for the life they desire: dream-setting, goal-setting, and building habits around individual goals.

Dream-setting is the act of clearly defining a dream. Dreams represent a vision of some future ideal state or reality. It's a two-step process:

1. Ask yourself what you want your ideal life to be ten, fifteen, or twenty years out. Then write down every detail of your ideal future life. Be very specific in the details: the income you earn, the house you live in, the boat you own, the car you drive, the money you've accumulated, etc. This is the future letter strategy that I referred to previously.

2. Using this detailed description of your ideal future life, make a bullet point list of each one of the details that represent your ideal life. These would be the income you earn, the house you live in, the boat your own, etc. These details represent your wishes or dreams.

In my research, I uncovered seven strategies that successful people use to create a blueprint for their perfect, ideal life. I call these the Future Mirror Strategies. Each one of these strategies represents a future, ideal state. Let me share them with you:

FUTURE MIRROR STRATEGIES

1. Your soul mate: Who do you want to spend the rest of your life with? What kind of person is your soul mate? Are they upbeat, enthusiastic, happy, and anxious to succeed in life? In a hundred words or less, paint a picture with words, exactly who and what this person is. What they look like; what they do for a living; who their friends are; their type of personality. Describe in intricate detail everything about this person you will share the rest of your life with.

2. Your career: What is your ideal job? How much money do you make? What type of people do you work with? What does your ideal work day look like? What exotic places does your ideal job take you? What skills do you acquire in your perfect career? Once again, try to keep it to a hundred words.

3. Your health: How much do you want to weigh? What shape are you in? What do you do to stay in shape? What types of food do you eat that keep you fit and trim? Once again, try to keep it to a hundred words.

4. Your home: What does your ideal home look like? Where do you live? How big is your home? How much money is it worth? How many rooms does it have? Describe those rooms. Describe your neighborhood. Leave nothing out. Again, keep to a hundred words.

5. Your activities: In your ideal life, what kind of extracurricular activities do you engage in every day, every weekend, on vacation, etc? These can be hobbies, side businesses, or activities that you are passionate about. Again, keep to a hundred words.

6. Your stuff: What things do you own? What kind of toys do you have? What car do you drive? What does your watch look like? How about your clothes? How much money do you have? How do you invest your wealth? Again, a hundred words is all you need.

7. The big picture: The final strategy requires that you pull it all together. In a thousand words or less, script your ideal life. Spare no details. Identify the specific people, career, health, home, toys, money, and goals achieved that you want as a part of your perfect life. This big picture will become the blueprint of your life. It gives you a clear picture of your destination.

After you have defined your "big picture" through this scripting process, the next step is to make a list of all of your dreams and wishes, by referring back to your "big picture" script of your ideal future life. This dream/wish list will be the springboard for creating specific goals around each one of your dreams.

Goal-Setting

Only after you've defined your wishes or dreams, does the goal-setting process begin. This goal-setting process requires you to build goals around each one of your wishes or dreams. In order to build goals around each wish or dream you need to ask yourself two questions:

1. What would I need to do, what activities would I need to engage in, in order for each wish or dream to come true?

2. Can I perform those activities?

If the answer to question two is yes, then those activities represent your goals. Goals are only goals when they involve physical action and you have the capability to successfully take action. For example, if your wish is to make $200,000, what would you need to do, in a given year, in order to make $200,000? What specific activities would you need to engage in successfully during a given year in order to make $200,000? Make more telemarketing phone calls? Do more training? Get a specific license in your industry? Expand your product offering? Purchase more rental properties? Invest in more efficient equipment or technology? Then you must ask yourself if you have the capability to do these things. Do you have the necessary knowledge and skills to take action? If you do, then each action you must take represents a goal. If you don't have the capability to act then you must develop that capability before you can even begin to pursue each individual goal.

Let me give you another example: Let's say you're a salesman and you want to increase your income by $50,000 a year. That $50,000 is a dream. What do you need to do in order for that dream to come true? What action steps must you accomplish in order to realize that $50,000? Let's break it down:

- How much is an average sale? Answer: $5,000
- What is your commission on each sale? Answer: $500
- How many sales will it take to reach $50,000? Answer: 100

- How do you go about prospecting for sales? Answer: making phone calls is the best method
- How many phone calls does it take for you to set up one sales meeting? Answer: five phone calls
- How many meetings does it take to close one sale? Answer: four meetings
- How many meetings will it take to reach $50,000? Answer: 400 meetings
- How many phone calls will it take to get those 400 meetings? Answer: 2,000
- How many days do you work each year? Answer: 250
- How many phone calls will you need to make each day to get those 400 meetings, 100 sales, and your additional $50,000? Answer: eight phone calls each day.

In order to make an additional $50,000 you will need to make eight phone calls each day—that's a new a daily habit. Can you make eight phone calls each day? If the answer is yes, then this is your daily habit: make eight phone calls each day.

Summary: Building Habits Around Individual Goals

Essentially, there's a two-step process to building a house:

1. Draw up blueprints
2. Construct the house

Seems pretty simple, doesn't it? Each component of your house must be defined in the blueprint and then built: the kitchen, bathrooms, family room, dining room, bedrooms, and anything else you want your house to have—those are the components of your house.

Constructing an ideal, happy, and successful life is no different. It's the same process. In the case of your ideal life, the components of your life's blueprint are all the things that make a perfect life: the job you want to have (what you would love to do for a living), the place you want to live, the life partner you'd like to share your life with, the places you'd like to travel to, the wealth you'd like to accumulate, etc. These are known as dreams or wishes. You start building your ideal life by defining all of your dreams and wishes, which when compiled together become the blueprint of your life.

Your goals are your construction team. You need to define all of the goals that will make all of your dreams and wishes become a reality. You design your goals around each dream or wish. One dream or wish could require the achievement of one, five, or ten goals. The realization of each dream or wish happens when you accomplish all of the goals that are required in order for each specific dream or wish to be realized.

You can automatically process certain activities into your day that will allow you to achieve your individual goals. These daily activities are your habits. You need to build daily habits around each goal. Habits put you on autopilot. They take the struggle out of achieving your goals. Put each daily habit on your to-do list and track the completion of those habits. This is what successful people do. They automate success. And habits are how they automate success every day.

Let's summarize this dream-setting, goal-setting, and habits-building process:

- Paint a picture with words of your ideal life.
- Define each dream or wish that must be realized in order to have your ideal future life.

- Establish specific goals around each one of your dreams or wishes.
- Build daily activities (habits) around each individual goal.

You then repeat this process for every other dream or wish.

CHANGING YOUR HABITS

IF YOU don't know what you're doing, changing just one habit is hard. Remember, the brain fights you when it comes to habit change. As a result, most newly formed habits fall apart after a few weeks. Also, when you end an old habit, after a few weeks the brain eventually forces you back into those old habits. Eventually, your motivation and willpower wears off or you become stressed and your old habits rear their heads. If you don't know the tricks to habit change you have to rely on something I call "extreme disgust" to force habit change. Extreme disgust is hard to come by. It's essentially hitting rock bottom—you are simply fed up with your life circumstances and you are able to muster an unusually powerful type of willpower that enables you to change your habits. But, as I said, that's unusual. You don't want to have to wait until your life falls apart because of your habits. You don't want to wait to hit rock bottom.

After more than eleven years of studying the habits of over three hundred and fifty wealthy and poor people, I uncovered certain principles on habit change that make the process infinitely easier. I created an easy-to-follow program that will give you the tools to change your habits in just twenty-one days. That's why you bought this book. You want a simple, easy-to-follow habit-change process in order to avoid getting to that rock bottom point in your life. In addition to this easy-to-follow process, I'm going to share with you the latest in habit change science that will enable you to trick your brain into changing your habits without putting up a fight. This is what you've been waiting for. The buildup is over. Now fasten your seat belts because your life is about to change in ways you could only have dreamed of. Let's get started.

Habit Awareness

In order to change your habits, you need to first become aware of them. Awareness requires tracking all of your habits, from the moment you wake up, to the moment you go to sleep. Two days of tracking is all it takes. You want to do this during the workweek because most habits are triggered by the environment and during periods of stress. The workplace is the most common source of stress. Below is an example of a Habit Awareness Schedule:

HABIT AWARENESS SCHEDULE

1	Wake up at 8 am to begin my day
2	Have a cup of coffee with a buttered bagel
3	Smoke a cigarette with my coffee
4	Shower and get ready for work
5	Commute to work in my car. Smoke a cigarette during my commute
6	Listen to music or talk radio during my commute
7	Check email and voicemail first thing at work
8	Respond to emails and voicemail first thing at work
9	Work
10	Take break, gossip with collegues for 15 minutes

11	Respond to emails and phone calls as they come in during morning
12	Lunch with colleagues at a fast food restaurant
13	Gossip during lunch
14	Work in the afternoon
15	Respond to emails and phone calls as they come in during afternoon
16	Take break, gossip with collegues, and grab a smoke for 15 minutes
17	Leave work at 5 pm
18	Commute home and listen to talk shows, the news, or music
19	Eat dinner, have a few beers or some wine
20	Watch TV for three hours
21	Read science fiction book in bed for an hour or more
22	Fall asleep between 11 to 11:30 pm

Use the blank schedule below to track your habits and create your own Habit Awareness Schedule.

HABIT AWARENESS SCHEDULE

1	
2	
3	
4	
5	
6	
7	
8	

9	
10	
11	
12	
13	
14	
15	
16	
17	
18	
19	
20	
21	
22	

Habit Grading

The next step in the habit change process is to grade the habits you currently have. Put a plus (+) next to good habits and a minus (–) next to bad habits. Here's an example:

HABIT GRADING SCHEDULE   + OR -

1	Wake up at 8 am to begin my day	-
2	Have a cup of coffee with a buttered bagel	-
3	Smoke a cigarette with my coffee	-
4	Shower and get ready for work	
5	Commute to work in my car. Smoke a cigarette during my commute	-

6	Listen to music or talk radio during my commute	-
7	Check email and voicemail first thing at work	-
8	Respond to emails and voicemail first thing at work	-
9	Work	+
10	Take break, gossip with collegues for 15 minutes	-
11	Respond to emails and phone calls as they come in during morning	-
12	Lunch with colleagues at a fast food restaurant	-
13	Gossip during lunch	-
14	Work in the afternoon	+
15	Respond to emails and phone calls as they come in during afternoon	-
16	Take break, gossip with collegues and grab a smoke for 15 minutes	-
17	Leave work at 5 pm	-
18	Commute from work and listen to talk shows, news or music	-
19	Eat dinner, have a few beers or some wine	-
20	Watch TV for three hours	-
21	Read science fiction book in bed for an hour or more	-
22	Fall asleep between 11 to 11:30 pm	-

Now create your own Habit Grading Schedule using the Habits Awareness Schedule you just created:

HABIT GRADING SCHEDULE		+ OR -
1		
2		

3		
4		
5		
6		
7		
8		
9		
10		
11		
12		
13		
14		
15		
16		
17		
18		
19		
20		
21		
22		

This Habit Grading Schedule is your springboard for changing your habits. Don't worry that most of your habits are bad habits. The purpose of this exercise is to become aware of your bad habits. Awareness comes first in the habit-change process. When you know which habits are holding you back, you have the information you need to transform your life. Most people, unfortunately, skip this step entirely and jump right into adding new habits. Millions do this every year when they set New Year's resolutions. They never become aware of the existing habits they have, which are creating the foundation for the life they have. Habit change requires that you eliminate bad habits and then add new good habits. The goal is to tip your individual Habit Seesaw in the right direction. In order to do that, you need to become aware of the habits you currently have, and then identify them as good or bad.

Rich Habits Checklists

Phase One: Morning Habits

Now that you have identified all of your good and bad habits, it's time to begin creating your own customized Rich Habits Checklist. This checklist will eventually become part of your new daily routine. Habit change is a process. It takes time. The best approach is to focus on changing a few simple habits first. Phase one in this process is to select some morning habits you would like to change over the next seven-day period. Here is an example:

RICH HABITS CHECKLIST - PHASE ONE: MORNING

I woke at 6 am this morning
I read for learning for thirty minutes this morning
I exercised for thirty minutes this morning
I prepared my to-do list this morning

During my commute to work I listened to audio books or a podcast this morning
I did not eat any junk food this morning
I did not repeatedly check my email this morning
I did 3 things this morning that were related to my personal goals

Rich Habits Tip: Forty-four percent of the wealthy, successful people in my Rich Habits Study woke up three hours or more before their work day began. This morning time was earmarked for self-education reading, exercise, and other activities such as pursuing a goal, pursuing a passion, planning their day, writing, working a side business they were passionate about, studying for night school, etc. Those early morning hours represent an investment you make in yourself, every day. Take some time to create your own Rich Habits Morning Checklist:

RICH HABITS CHECKLIST

PHASE ONE: MORNING	S	M	T	W	T	F	S

RICH HABITS CHECKLIST

PHASE ONE: MORNING	S	M	T	W	T	F	S

For the next seven days this becomes your own customized Rich Habits Morning Checklist. Each day, check off every new rich habit you follow. This checklist will help force accountability in following your new morning rich habits. After seven days, these habits will begin to take root, creating synapses inside your brain that grow stronger every time you repeat each new habit. If you are able to check off 30 percent or more of your new habits, pat yourself on the back. It's important to understand that just changing a handful of your daily habits will have a profound impact on your life.

Phase Two: Daytime Habits

After following your Rich Habits Morning Checklist for at least seven days, you are now ready to move on to the next phase, changing your daytime habits using the same rich habits process. Here is an example:

RICH HABITS CHECKLIST - PHASE TWO: DAYTIME

I read for learning for thirty minutes during lunch or I worked on goal-related tasks during lunch
I did not gossip with fellow workers during lunch or in the afternoon
I did not eat any junk food at lunch or in the afternoon
I checked and responded to email/voicemail from 1 to 2 pm
During my commute from work I listened to audio books or a podcast
I drank a glass of water instead of coffee this afternoon
I made some hello calls, happy birthday calls, or life event calls this afternoon
I did two things this afternoon that were related to my personal goals

Rich Habits Tip: Sixty-three percent of the wealthy individuals in my study listened to audio books or podcasts during their commute to and from work. Ninety-five percent of the poor individuals in my study listened to radio talk shows or music during their commute. Seventy-nine percent of the wealthy individuals in my study did not smoke cigarettes, while 46 percent of the poor did. Gossip almost always is negative. Ninety-four percent of the wealthy in my study did not engage in gossip, while 79 percent of the poor in my study engaged in gossip on a daily basis. Seventy percent of the wealthy in my study ate less than three hundred junk food calories a day, while 97 percent of the poor in my study ate more than three hundred junk calories a day. The wealthy in my study dedicated specific time slots for responding to email and voicemail. This allowed them to focus on being productive, helping them avoid distractions. The poor in my study responded to email and voicemail throughout the day.

Take some time to now create your own Rich Habits Daytime Checklist:

RICH HABITS CHECKLIST PHASE TWO: DAYTIME	S	M	T	W	T	F	S

RICH HABITS CHECKLIST
PHASE TWO: DAYTIME

	S	M	T	W	T	F	S

Once again, you want to devote at least seven days to following your new daytime habits. Continue to follow your morning habits while simultaneously working on incorporating these new daytime habits into your routine. You may want to consolidate both the new morning and daytime habits.

Phase Three: Nighttime Habits

After another seven days, you are ready for phase three. In phase three you will be adding new nighttime habits to your daily routine. Once again, the springboard for creating your new nighttime habits will be the Habit Awareness Schedule you completed earlier. Here is an example:

RICH HABITS CHECKLIST - PHASE THREE: NIGHTTIME

I watched less than one hour of TV tonight
I spent less than one hour on recreational Internet tonight
I spent one hour or more pursuing a dream, goal, or developing a side business or marketable skill

I met with my networking group, nonprofit group, or business group tonight
I coached my son's sports team tonight
I did thirty minutes of self-education reading tonight
I got to bed no later than 10 pm tonight

Rich Habits Tip: Sixty-seven percent of the wealthy in my study watched less than one hour of TV each day while 77 percent of the poor in my study watched more than one hour of TV each day. Sixty-three percent of the wealthy in my study spent less than one hour each day on recreational Internet use, while 74 percent of the poor in my study spent more than one hour a day on the Internet recreationally, visiting sites like Facebook, YouTube, or Twitter. Sixty-two percent of the wealthy in my study devoted time every day to pursuing some goal, verses only 6 percent of the poor. Getting at least seven to eight hours of sleep every night is critical for your health, particularly brain health. The wealthy in my study averaged about seven and a half hours of sleep a night, while the poor averaged less than seven hours.

Take some time to now create your own Rich Habits Nighttime Checklist:

RICH HABITS CHECKLIST

PHASE THREE: NIGHTTIME	S	M	T	W	T	F	S

RICH HABITS CHECKLIST
PHASE THREE: NIGHTTIME

	S	M	T	W	T	F	S

Once again, you want to devote at least seven days to following your new nighttime habits. Continue to follow your morning and daytime habits, while simultaneously working on incorporating these new nighttime habits into your routine.

Consolidating Your New Habits

You may want to consolidate all of your new habits on the following schedule:

RICH HABITS CHECKLIST CONSOLIDATED	S	M	T	W	T	F	S

Once your Consolidated Rich Habits Checklist is complete, use it every day to hold yourself accountable. Over time, your new rich habits will become automatic. They will not require any willpower or thought. These habits will create a foundation for success in your life. They will pay dividends that will dramatically improve your financial circumstances, make you more confident, and automatically put you on a path toward success. They are an investment in you, in your growth, and in your happiness. Think of your rich habits as snowflakes on a mountainside. Over time your rich habits, like snowflakes, will accumulate. You will not notice the accumulation from day to day, but at some point they will create an avalanche; an avalanche of success. It might be a bonus, raise, promotion, better job, big customer or clients, or simply better health.

Shortcuts to Habit Change

There are six powerful shortcuts to habit change that speed up the process: merging habits, enacting the law of association, changing your environment, starting small, scheduling your new habits, and firewalling your bad habits. Each one of these makes habit change easier, quicker, and requires less willpower.

Merging Habits

Think of an existing habit (existing neural pathway) as a train on a track, except it's inside your brain. If you add your new habit to that same train, as if it were a new passenger, the brain won't put up a fight because you're not trying to take control of the train or the track. You're just taking a ride. When an old habit does not perceive a new habit as a threat, it does not wage war against the formation of the new habit.

Here's how it works: Let's say you want to add a new rich habit of self-education reading thirty minutes every day, and let's say you have an old habit of exercising on the StairMaster thirty minutes every day. If you were to put a book on the StairMaster and read that book while you're exercising, you will, almost immediately, form a new joint habit that sticks. The trigger for the habit will be the book on your StairMaster.

Here's another example: If you have an old habit of drinking coffee every day and you want to add a new rich habit of drinking a glass of water every day, you will put your coffee cup on a water cooler or in your sink or in your refrigerator, next to the water bottle. When your brain tells you it's time to drink coffee, you will, initially, search for your coffee cup. That coffee cup will then become a trigger, reminding you to drink a cup of water. That new joint habit will only take a few days to stick.

Enacting the Law of Association

Old habits can be triggered by the individuals you associate with. If you are trying to get rid of some old, bad habits, you need to limit the time you spend associating with those individuals who act as a trigger for those bad habits and begin associating with individuals who possess the new good habits you are trying to adopt. You can find these new individuals in network groups, non-profit groups, trade groups, or any group that is focused on pursuing similar goals. For example, if one of your new goals is to read more, you can join a reading group that meets periodically to discuss books the group reads. Another example would be finding individuals who run, jog, or exercise and begin jogging, running, or exercising with them. Once you open your eyes to habit change, you will begin to see that there are many individuals who have those same habits. They are all around you. You only begin to notice them after you make a decision to change your daily habits.

Changing Your Environment

It is much easier to abandon old habits and form new habits when your environment changes. New home, new neighbors, new friends, new job, new colleagues, new cities, etc., all offer an opportunity to forge new habits. When your environment changes, you are forced to think your way through each day. Spoons, knives, and forks are no longer where they used to be, so you have to think. Your commute to work is different, so you have to think. Your new responsibilities at work are different, so you have to think. Eventually your brain will force you to develop habits in your new environment in order to make the brain's job easier.

Starting Small

It is far easier to change your habits if you start with small habits. Small habit change involves adding habits that require very little effort. Examples include drinking more water during the day, taking vitamin supplements, or listening to audio books while you commute to work. Small habit change also includes cutting back on existing bad habits. Examples include reducing the number of cigarettes you smoke, reducing the amount of TV you watch by thirty minutes each day, or reducing your Facebook or Internet use to less than an hour a day. The smaller, easier the habit change the higher probability it will stick. Small habit change gives you momentum and increased confidence. This allows you to take on bigger, more complex habit changes in the future.

Scheduling Your New Habits

Sixty-seven percent of self-made millionaires in my study maintained a to-do list. To-do lists are a way of processing success into your life. One of the tricks self-made million-aires use is to incorporate certain good daily habits onto their to-do list. These specific daily habits show up automatically, every day, on their to-do lists. This forces accountability. Every day you must be accountable for the new daily habits you are trying to form. If they are simple daily habits, after a few weeks you won't need to include them on your to-do list—they will have become habits. You can then move on to other, new daily habits using this to-do list habit process.

Firewalling Your Bad Habits

One trick to habit change is to make it harder for you to engage in a bad habit by creating some type of firewall between you and the bad habit. For example, let's say you eat junk food late at night while watching TV. You eat that junk food because it's in your pantry. If it wasn't in your pantry you wouldn't be able to eat it. The way to make this bad habit harder to engage in, would be to stop stocking your pantry with junk food and instead stock your pantry with healthy snacks. The habit isn't eating junk food; the habit is snacking while you watch TV. Eliminating junk food may stop you from snacking, but more likely, when you sit to watch TV, the cue, you will default into your routine of seeking a snack. This time, however, the reward will be a different snack, ideally a healthy one or at least a low-calorie substitute.

Another bad habit might be spending hours on Facebook at night, after dinner. One way to make this habit harder to engage in would be to turn off your computer, or move your computer into the basement, or disconnect it from the router. Because it requires exerting some effort to engage in the bad habit, you won't, if your willpower is weak. And willpower is usually at its weakest at the end of the day.

CASE STUDIES: RICH HABITS AT WORK

Dr. Ben Carson: Read for Self-Improvement Daily

Ben Carson is a world-famous neurologist who was raised in one of Detroit's ghettos. His mom was afraid that her son would become just another casualty of ghetto life. To prevent this, Mrs. Carson made young Carson read every day for self-education. To ensure her son did his daily reading, she also required that he write a one-page summary about what he read each week so she could read it. Each day, young Carson would go to the library and spend hours reading. At the end of the week he would hand a summary of what he read that week to his mom for her to review. This daily reading rich habit opened Dr. Carson's eyes. He read stories about the lives of other poor, self-made millionaires. He began to think that if they could rise from poverty to wealth, so could he. Eventually, this daily reading became a habit that helped inspire Dr. Carson to try harder in school. As his grades improved, he gained confidence. This confidence made him believe that he could go to college, then on to medical school to become a doctor. He continued to read and learn every day throughout his adult life. Eventually, he became one of the most famous and respected neurosurgeons in the world. What I find most interesting about this story is that many years after his mom forced this reading rich habit on him, Dr. Carson learned that his mom was illiterate. She never actually could read any of his weekly summaries. Intuitively, Mrs. Carson knew that if she could instill in her son the daily rich habit of reading it would help get him out of the ghetto and set him up for success in life. And it worked!

Arnold Schwarzenegger: Pursue Your Dreams

Arnold Schwarzenegger first gained international celebrity as a professional body builder and then went on to become a Hollywood celebrity and politician. But it all started for Arnold when, as a teenager, he stumbled upon a magazine featuring Reg Park, the famous actor who played Hercules in a very popular Italian movie series that began back in 1961. Inspired by Park, Arnold began working out with weights, and his dream of becoming the world's greatest bodybuilder was born. Arnold's single-minded focus on realizing his dream is legendary. Two months prior to a Mr. Olympia body-building contest, Arnold's father died. His mother pleaded with him to return to Austria to attend the funeral. Arnold said no. He told his mom it would distract him from his training. Years later, Arnold would confess that his decision, although the right one for him because he won the title, damaged his relationship with his mother and his girlfriend at the time. Neither could understand how his dream took precedence over the death of his father. But Arnold's dream did take precedence. It took precedence over every part of his life. Arnold picked up his first barbell in 1960. Ten years later he earned his first Mr. Olympia title. Ten years dedicated to pursuing one singular dream. Arnold would apply his laser-like focus in pursuing other dreams, such as becoming a famous actor and, much later in life, governor of California. While Arnold is an extreme example of focus, his story does highlight the importance of a single-minded focus in pursuing your dreams.

Richard Branson: Create Multiple Streams of Income

Richard Branson is one of the most fascinating self-made millionaires of the twenty-first century. He puts the rich habit of having multiple streams of income on steroids. Branson does not rely on any single source of income. He has hundreds. Branson started and grew four hundred companies in a vast array of industries that includes: music retail, music record label, music video production, international airline, rugby team, spacecraft manufacturer, telecommunications, mobile phones, fitness centers, book retail, book publishing, book distribution, alternative energy, banking, venture capital, travel agencies, hotels, ski lodge, spas, passenger bikes, racing team, radio, railway, and many others. What makes Branson unique is that he has failed often, made thousands of mistakes, and yet, despite those failures and mistakes, remains fearless and passionate about pursuing every challenge and every new opportunity. His desire to expand the Virgin brand is really a desire to expand his streams of income. Branson learned very early on that this rich habit creates the most wealth.

Robin Sharma: Get Up Early

Robin Sharma is a world-renown leadership expert, personal and professional development coach, consultant to Fortune 500 Companies, professional motivational speaker, and bestselling author with over six million books sold. Sharma attributes much of his success to the rich habit of waking up early. He likes to call his early morning routine the "5 AM Club." This is the time of day Sharma gets in his exercise, reading, meditating, and prep work for his day. This singular rich habit has created a wealth empire for Sharma that makes him one of the most famous leadership experts in the world.

Jack Canfield: Find a Mentor

Jack Canfield, author of the Chicken Soup for the Soul series and *Success Principles*, holds the Guinness World Record for most books sold by an author: 500 million. He is also considered the number one success coach in America. His seminars, training programs, and coaching programs teach tens of thousands his success principles each year. How did he do it? Canfield was mentored by C. Clement Stone, a legendary personal development expert who also mentored Og Mandino, a former publisher of *SUCCESS Magazine* and author of *The Greatest Salesmen in the World*, a book that sold over 20 million copies. But Clement was only one of Canfield's mentors in life. Others who helped mentor Canfield include: Mark Victor Hansen, Janet Switzer, John Gray, Bob Proctor, Jim Rohn, and John Maxwell. That's a lot of mentors!

APPENDIX: RICH HABITS TRACKING SCHEDULE

BEG WEIGHT	
GOAL WEIGHT	
END WEIGHT	
CALORIES GOAL	

DATE	DAY OF WEEK	WEIGHT	# OF CARDIO MINUTES	# OF GYM MINUTES	BREAKFAST CALORIES	LUNCH CALORIES	DINNER CALORIES	TOTAL CALORIES TODAY	CUMULATIVE CALORIES FOR MONTH	AVERAGE CALORIES
									–	–
									–	–
									–	–
									–	–
									–	–
									–	–
									–	–
									–	–
									–	–

MONTH	CARDIO DAYS	MIN	GYM DAYS	AVG CALORIES	LBS (LOST)/GAIN	BEG WEIGHT	END WEIGHT
JANUARY							
FEBRUARY					-		
MARCH					-		
APRIL					-		
MAY					-		
JUNE					-		
JULY							
AUGUST							
SEPTEMBER							
OCTOBER					-		
NOVEMBER					-		
DECEMBER							

ABOUT THE AUTHOR

Tom Corley understands the difference between being rich and poor: at age nine, his family went from being multi-millionaires to broke in just one night. As an adult, for five years, Tom observed and documented the daily activities of two hundred and thirty-three wealthy people and one hundred and twenty-eight people struggling with poverty. He discovered there is an immense difference between the habits of the wealthy, particularly self-made millionaires, and the poor. During his research he identified over three hundred daily activities that separated the "haves" from the "have-nots." The culmination of his research can be found in his number one, bestselling book, *Rich Habits: The Daily Success Habits of Wealthy Individuals*.

A dynamic and empowering speaker, Tom travels the world, motivating audiences at industry conferences, corporate events, universities, multi-level marketing group events, and global sales organizations' presentations. He has spoken on the same stage with many famous entrepreneurs and personal development experts, such as Richard Branson, Robin Sharma, Dr. Daniel Amen, and many others.

Tom has shared his insights on various national and international network, cable, and Internet television programs such as CBS Evening News, Yahoo Financially Fit, Money.com, India TV, News.com Australia, and a host of others. He has wowed listeners on many prestigious nationally syndicated radio shows, including the Dave Ramsey Show, Marketplace Money, and WABC.

Featured in numerous print magazines—such as *Money* magazine, *Inc. Magazine*, *SUCCESS Magazine*, *Entrepreneur* magazine, *More* magazine, and *Kiplinger's Personal Finance* magazine—and various online publications, including USA Today, CNN, MSN Money, SUCCESS.com, Inc.com, and the Huffington Post. Tom is also a frequent contributor to Credit.com and *Business Insider*.

National publicity has garnered international media attention for Tom and his rich habits research. Broadcast media, online publications, and television throughout Asia, the South Pacific, Europe, the United Kingdom, and Central and South America have supported Tom's powerful message.

In an effort to help adults instill good habits in the younger generation, Tom released his second book, *Rich Kids: How to Raise Our Children to be Happy and Successful in Life*. This book was the self-help category winner of the 2015 New York Book Festival.

Tom is also a CPA, CFP, and holds a master's degree in taxation. As president of Cerefice and Company, CPAs, Tom heads one of the premier financial firms in New Jersey.

INDEX